==================

DiDiYumYum
and the
Mad Yank

A Love Story By
David Kujawa

=================================

In Memory Of
My Darling Diane
I'll never find another you

"We loved with a love that was
more than love." – Edgar Allan Poe

INTRODUCTION – NON, JE NE REGRETTE RIEN

My life has been rather neatly divided into two distinct halves – Before Diane and With Diane. We came together at roughly the midway point in our lives and we both had quite varied and interesting lives before then. But it was the second half – our more than thirty-five years of shared existence – that was infinitely better. I suppose that I have had three major obsessions in my life – writing, movies and sex, not necessarily in that order. In many ways, Diane became my fourth obsession. No one ever affected me the way she did.

Our wonderful life together came to a sudden and unexpected end on 10 February 2020 when Diane passed away peacefully in her sleep. It was the worst day of my life and one from which I will never totally recover. I am left feeling lost and empty. We had said goodnight the night before but we never said goodbye.

Writing has always been a kind of therapy for me so now, more than a year later, I have embarked upon this book, not knowing where it will lead me or even if I will be able to finish it. I want it to be a sort of memorial to Diane but my main purpose is to preserve the memories of our life together before time and age make them fade. Some years ago, I wrote a book about our various travels around Europe with a similar purpose in mind – to keep our memories. We would occasionally dip into it and the pictures and anecdotes helped us to recall moments that we might had otherwise forgotten. Life is made up of the times we remember.

This then is our story, hopefully told with both honesty and humour. It is, of course, a love story but also the story of two very different people who complemented one another and changed each other's lives for the better.

======================================

ONE - DAVID

Probably the best way to begin at the beginning would be to provide some background into the lives of Diane and David in the years before we even knew each other existed.

I was born at an early age in Baltimore way back in 1948 and thus qualified to be a baby boomer. My family was Polish American – I never heard my maternal grandparents speak anything but Polish – although by the time my generation arrived we were far more American than Polish. I was the third of four children – a typical position for a troublesome or rebellious child. My two brothers were seven and five years older than me while my sister was three years younger.

My family, sometime in the mid-1950s. I'm the little guy standing.

Ours was not a particularly warm family. Displays of affection, except between our parents, were rare. We were all given a Catholic education and, as a result, my siblings became and remain very religious. In this regard, as in many other things, I was quietly resistant. My mother was strict and liked us to maintain an orderly existence. I remember that on the first day we moved into our new house she assigned each of us a specific place at the dining room table and we never once altered that seating plan. There was a strange sort of formality in our home environment. One of my girlfriends, on a rare visit to the house, remarked how my siblings and I, in talking about our parents, always referred to them as "our father" and "our mother" instead of Dad and Mom.

My father worked very hard, including several evenings, as an insurance salesman so our contact with him was largely limited to weekends and vacations. I think my mother was a trifle obsessive-compulsive in her fixed ways of doing things. She also did not approve of a great many things, most of which were the things that would eventually appeal to me.

Perhaps as a form of escape or because I was primarily a solitary creature, I fell in love with the movies at an early age and would rather be in a movie theatre than anywhere. In the summer months, when other kids were outside playing, I never had a tan because I preferred to spend my afternoons in the darkened picture palaces. My boyhood hero was Errol Flynn who I came to know through old movies shown on television. It was the influence of movies that led me to start writing my own stories at the age of eleven.

It was about this time that I became an ardent Anglophile. It started with seeing Peter Sellers in *The Mouse That Roared* and led to my discovery on the radio of *The Goon Show* and then on to just about everything British. The advent of the Beatles and the Swinging Sixties would only fuel my obsession. I used to say that Baltimore was a big city with a small town mentality and all this wonderful stuff I was being exposed to only reinforced that opinion.

Although I was supposedly intelligent with a good IQ, I was never a very good student. School always seemed to interfere with the things I really wanted to do. Even so, I managed to get into one of the best public high schools – the same one my brothers had gone to – where the highlight of my scholastic life was my involvement in the school's dramatics. It was where I wrote my first plays and saw them performed. At the same time, I got involved with a professional repertory theatre just down the street from the school. This was to be the beginning of my emergence from my introverted shell and becoming my own person. My parents, needless to say, were far from pleased.

I was just the right age to appreciate all the changes that came during the Sixties. In 1965, I started my first job at the public library while still going to school and doing odd bits at the theatre. A couple of years later I left school and the job became full time. I exerted my independence my getting my own downtown apartment at an age when most guys were thinking about their first car. It is probably a result of this preference that I never got a driver's license.

It was while working at the library that I met my first wife – Jackie. She was not the only girl I went out with but we had an on and off relationship that kept bringing us back together. During one of these spells of togetherness, Jackie announced that she was pregnant. Since we were both Catholics – albeit lapsed ones – it seemed that marriage was inevitable. Nowadays that hardly seems to be the case – in fact, it seems to be quite normal. But in 1970, an unmarried Catholic girl with a baby was considered a scandal. So Jackie and I got married. In retrospect, it was the worst decision I ever made.

My son Nicholas was born on 13 February 1971 in the same hospital where I had been born and where Jackie worked as a lab technician. I do not think that either of us was really cut out to be parents but we tried our best. I had left the library and now worked in the music business, eventually becoming the warehouse manager for a chain of record shops. After a while, Jackie went back to work and, after two or three years of struggling, we achieved a relatively comfortable lifestyle. But it was hardly a case of living happily ever after.

We both grew restless, especially Jackie who had previously been quite a popular party girl. I think we must have both looked at one another and thought: "Is this it?" So, as the permissive Seventies progressed, we evolved into having what was then known as an open marriage. It had its advantages and disadvantages. It certainly seemed to indicate that whatever Jackie and I felt for each other was not necessarily true love. At first, we lived the cliché of staying together because we had a young child. But as Nicholas got older and became aware of the tension between us, even that excuse sounded hollow.

Jackie eventually found that she had a talent for belly dancing which had begun as a hobby and form of exercise. This soon developed into public performances into which I was dragged and it almost seemed like we had found something to bring us back together. But then she started to do "bellygrams" for a singing telegram company – for which she did not need me – and the habit of her being out very late several nights a week began. It was hard to think of us as being a couple.

I confess to having my own set of vices. I started smoking when I was in high school because just about all of the people I admired in the movies smoked. I even tried smoking a pipe for a while but decided it was too much trouble. Amazingly, I got through the entire decade of the Sixties without ever experimenting with drugs. This was because alcohol was the drug of choice for the people I associated with, both at work and in the theatre. No doubt there were drugs around and easily available – mostly pot – but I was never tempted. Instead

I consumed lots of vodka, often to excess. I somehow progressed from being a fairly happy drunk to an annoying one. Once, at a party, I was chucked outside and ended up face down in the snow because I was not behaving well. I had also inherited my father's quick temper which worried me. So, at some point in 1976 or 1977, I totally gave up drinking and soon found that I did not miss it. The only drink I have had since then was a sip of champagne when I married Diane.

One day while having lunch in the records warehouse and reading through the latest copy of *Rolling Stone,* I found a small ad in the back pages for prospective "English Rose" pen friends. The Anglophile in me was intrigued and I promptly sent off for more information. After paying a small fee, I received the names and addresses of five English girls who wanted to correspond with American guys. One of them was Diane.

===

TWO - DIANE

I have been able to put together some details of Diane's earlier life from various sources, some more reliable than others, and from the memories she used to share with me over the years. When the mood hit us, we would sit and talk for hours about our childhoods, school days and other experiences and marvel at how different our lives had been. One idea that popped up from time to time was whether we would have liked each other if we had met earlier, say in the Seventies. Of course, it was a running joke with Diane that she could remember very little from the Seventies but I think there were certain things she simply did not want to talk about. Even so, we were quite open with one another during these reminiscences and a few inhibitions had a habit of becoming looser as the clock crept into the early hours.

Diane was born in London on 27 March 1950. She was the second daughter of Annie and Ron Cockerton – her sister Lynne was about two years older. Diane began to demonstrate an unpredictable nature at an early age. Lynne once said that she was regarded as the good girl but Diane was "the one" who required careful supervision. Diane told me that she had to be given an unbreakable cup when drinking because she would simply drop it on the floor when she was finished. When the family went to the beach, Diane was adamant that no grains of sand were allowed on her blanket. I recently came across an old black and white and slightly blurred photo of Diane aged about five or six. She is running on a beach in her bathing suit with a worried look on her face. On the back of the photo, her mother had written: "Diane in trouble (as usual)". By all accounts, she was quite a handful and yet she could also be painfully shy with strangers, something she never completely got over.

It is not surprising that, because of her nature, Diane was bullied at school. One of my favourite early Diane stories is about her finally snapping after persistent bullying by "a stupid, fat ugly girl" and pushing the unpleasant brat down an entire flight of stairs. There was a hint of pride in Diane's voice when she told me this story and I felt that it was an important moment in her young life.

The Cockerton family – Diane is on the left.
The girl on the right is (I think) a friend of Lynne's.

Despite such problems, Diane apparently loved going to school and spoke fondly about a couple of the teachers who took an interest in her. Unfortunately, her education suffered a setback when she developed Type 1 diabetes. She had a rough time of it as the family doctor misinterpreted the symptoms and it was only her mother's insistence that she be taken into hospital where the condition was confirmed. By this time, she needed a lengthy stay to bring it under control. For some reason, I always thought this happened when Diane was about sixteen and she never did anything to correct this impression. But when I went through some of her old school papers (it is amazing some of the stuff she kept) they indicated a long absence due to sickness when she was thirteen. Either way, it was something she was going to have to live with.

The Cockertons began taking holidays to the Continent when Diane was ten – before the big tourist boom when English travellers were greeted more as a novelty than a nuisance. They went in a converted Bedford van which Ron had fitted out himself and stayed in campsites rather than hotels which was really roughing it compared to my American vacations. Their first trip was to Biarritz and for the following years they gradually explored farther afield, usually staying in campsites on the coast and, as Diane fondly recalled, preferably where it was hot. Sometimes they were accompanied by various family members and, on at least one occasion, by a friend of Lynne's. They saw the small villages and seaside towns when they were still relatively unspoilt. So Diane was exposed to an international atmosphere at an early age and developed a love of travel that she never lost. She related stories about playing with kids from other countries even though there was no common language. It all sounded wonderful.

Diane's family was totally different from mine. They were warm and loving even if Dad, a long distance lorry driver at the time, was not always there. Diane and her mother became very close even though Diane sometimes put Annie through an emotional ringer with her various antics.

She could not wait to start dating and her mid-teen years were devoted to a boy named Michael who she always said was prettier than she was. The relationship sadly ended in tears when Diane was seventeen but it did not entirely cure her of romance.

I love this picture of young Diane.
I wonder what she would have thought of me then.

Instead of going to college, Diane trained for a career as a secretary. She also had a very active social life – it was the Swinging Sixties after all. She loved the music and the dancing and the fashions – there is one lovely photo of her in a miniskirt – and she loved boys. Diane frequently did things to excess. By this time she was a regular smoker and it was a habit that would only get worse as the years went by.

By the time we get to the 1970s, things become complicated and vague. Diane's sister had married a chap named Brian who was a bit of an entrepreneur. He wanted to set up home and business in the wilds of Hampshire near the New Forest and he wanted Diane's parents to come as well. Apparently, the invitation also extended to Diane but she preferred to remain in London. Somewhere in the midst of all this, Diane had also got married to someone called Tony Williams. This period of her life is among the vague ones. The marriage did not last very long – Diane always said it was about a year – and the divorce was final in February 1975.

Diane never talked much about Tony Williams. If she had any idea what happened to him after the divorce, she never let on. But it was soon after Williams made his exit (if not before) that the major character of Gerry van Dongen made his entrance.

Gerry was allegedly Diane's soul mate. She loved him madly even though he was not always very nice to her. They seem to have had a somewhat stormy relationship. Gerry was of Dutch descent who sometimes worked with his father as a carpenter making reproduction furniture. But he mostly lived life on the edge. He was a drug user and occasional dealer who introduced Diane to harder stuff than pot. He was probably also a petty criminal, emphasis on petty. Diane said that Gerry always thought he was smarter than everyone else. The problem was he was often out of his head with drink and drugs. I once asked Diane what attracted her to Gerry and got little more than a shrug in reply.

I often thought that Gerry and Jackie would make a wonderful couple.

In a possible effort to prove their hippy credentials, Diane and Gerry once spent the month of September hitchhiking through the Netherlands and Germany. It was Gerry's intention to eventually reach Australia but Diane had dreams of going to India. She had even booked a return trip for herself on a Magic Bus from Bombay to London. But by the time they reached the border with Austria the weather had become so bad with what they were told were the worst blizzards in years that they gave up and returned to England where Diane once again found a secretarial job.

At some point, Gerry persuaded Diane to quit her job (she was the only one who was ever in steady employment) and to join him and another couple on another hippie-type journey through Europe that would ultimately last six months. Travelling in what Diane always described as "an old Hillman", they first went to France where they worked for a time picking grapes on a large vineyard ("bloody hard work" Diane recalled) apparently in return for meals and lodging in a workers' hostel. I have no idea how long this lasted but they eventually continued through France and into Spain. They slept in tents beside the Hillman and caught fish and managed to acquire supplies including, of course, the all-important drugs.

The only surviving photo of Diane's hippie adventure
Taken in Valencia, October 1977

Somehow they ended up in Morocco and not necessarily in the touristy bits. I often wonder how much of this part of the story Diane exaggerated or simply could not remember clearly. There was the anecdote about a very primitive public convenience that was surrounded by barbed wire and had an armed guard to whom an entrance fee had to be paid. Then there was the seedy nightclub where Gerry and his mate were supposedly offered all the drugs they wanted in exchange for the two girls.

Whatever the reality, this adventure seemed to have a profound effect on Diane and she mentioned it often, usually in quite a wistful way. Coming back to England and reality must have been a real jolt. Diane was a strange sort of hippie who could maintain a secretarial job during the day (in a miniskirt of course) and completely let loose in the evenings and on weekends. She loved rock music and she and Gerry and their friends often went to some of the big rock festivals such as Reading and Knebworth where Diane was supposedly very quick to take her top off.

She and Gerry had a flat above some shops in the Essex town of Brentwood and this flat became a kind of mecca for the local dropouts and deadheads who all seemed to know Gerry. It was not unusual for Diane to come home from work and be expected to cook for six to eight people. Again, the only apparent reason she put up with everything was because she was also out of her head much of the time.

I once asked Diane how she managed to cope with her diabetes in these conditions. She had no real answer other than to say that if her blood sugar levels went low and she had a hypo, the others just left her alone and assumed she would eventually come out of it naturally. I kind of doubt that – I would have thought that at least some of the girls would have been more helpful or sympathetic.

Things got out of hand at a party one night when one of the deadheads got into an argument with Diane and slapped her. In retaliation, Gerry went into the kitchen, got a knife, and stabbed the guy. It was not a fatal wound but it was enough to get Gerry into some very serious trouble. It seemed prison was a likely outcome so it was suggested that some leniecy might be possible if Gerry could be presented as a married man. As a result, Diane married him in February 1978. It did not save him for prison.

Again, Diane resisted the offer to move to Hampshire to live with her family. She was determined to keep going where she was. She soon landed a very good job as a legal secretary at the highly regarded firm of Norton Rose Botterell Roche (later simply Norton Rose) where she would work for twenty-five years.

When Gerry was released, he was different and bitter. In typical male fashion, he took out his anger and frustration on someone close to him – Diane. He was abusive, both physically and verbally, and completely eroded her fragile self confidence. He made Diane think that she had to stay with him because no one else would want her. He took most of her money and sometimes would disappear for days at a time. The breaking point came when Gerry had an affair with a friend of Diane's who had come to stay with her. Supposedly, this creature said to Diane: "Mind if I borrow your husband?"

It took all of Diane's strength to leave Gerry. At first she sought refuge with friends but one of these turned out to be even worse than her husband when it came to abuse. In desperation, Diane swallowed a bunch of pills. She, of course, survived and after being released from hospital finally went to stay with Mum and Dad in Hampshire. She several times told me the story of being in the kitchen with her mother and Annie remarking: "Today would have been your funeral" which caused both of them to break down in uncontrollable tears.

Despite Gerry's pleadings for Diane to take him back and his promises never to do it again, she was finally divorced from him in December 1982. By this time she had already found an American pen friend.

THREE – PEN FRIENDS

It is impossible to know what fate or gods caused Diane and me to experiment with transatlantic correspondence in early 1982 as possibly a distraction or an escape from the emptiness both of us were feeling. Maybe we both needed someone new to talk to and there seemed to be something safe about having one or more long distance pen friends. Whatever the reason, I took the plunge and wrote the following letter to Diane who at that time was nothing more than a name and address I had been given.

Dear Diane –

I received your name through Harmony as a possible pen friend whose interests are similar to my own. I hope we will be able to become good friends through our correspondence.

It's always difficult to know how to begin a letter to someone you've never met. I suppose the best thing would be for me to tell you a bit about myself. I'm 34 years old and have lived most of my life here in Baltimore. I am of Polish descent although my last name is sometimes mistaken for Japanese, Indian, African and a lot of other things. I work for a chain of record shops as a warehouse manager. My job also involves overseeing the various store inventories, paperwork and dealing with the record companies. Since I enjoy all types of music immensely, the job has obvious advantages in its contant exposure to the music scene.

Originally, in my more carefree and idealistic youth, I had hoped for a career in the theatre. I worked for several years with a couple of professional rep companies both as an actor and an "A.S.M." (assistant stage manager – a polite way of saying that my duties were all the little backstage jobs that no one else wanted to do). But my real ambition was (is?) to be a playwright. Over the years I produced a stack of scripts that have curiously managed to avoid any form of production.

So now my association with the theatre is limited mainly to being a member of the audience. Baltimore, as you might suspect, is hardly one of the great cultural centers of the country. But, happily, it is less than a ninety minute drive to Washington which does have a number of good theatres, especially the Kennedy Center. Thus I am able to indulge my tastes for drama, ballet, music and even old films. At least until Reagan cuts everybody's budget into oblivion.

I suppose I'm what has been called an Anglophile. I've loved British films and plays and music for years. I became addicted to the Goon Show at the age of twelve (much to the horror of my family). And my own writing shows the definite influence of some of my favorite writers: Osborne, Pinter, Stoppard, Simon Gray, Frederic Raphael – although not all at the same time, of course. And when the Beatles and all the other British bands invaded our shores in the sixties, I was in ecstasy, Even today, the majority of the television I watch are British series and shows imported by our public broadcasting stations.

All of which is why the idea of having a pen friend in England is such an intriguing one. I don't know why I've never thought of it before. But now that I have, I hope we'll be able to share all sorts of ideas and interests with one another. I'm looking forward to finding out what things are really like on the other side of the Atlantic.

So do write and tell me all about yourself – or at least make a start. And please forgive my typing a personal letter. My handwriting is nearly impossible to decipher – even by me at times. But if you would prefer the pen to the machine, I can only promise to do my best.

I don't really know what else to say at this point. Except that I'll be looking forward to hearing from you. Until then, take very good care of yourself.

Vry trly yrs,

David

The observant reader will no doubt notice that I did not mention the fact that I was married. This was not necessarily being evasive or deceptive. I never thought that anything romantic would ever come out of this letter writing – I was genuinely only interested in communicating with someone in England. The fact that this friend was female was down to two reasons: (1) I always got on much better with women than men, and (2) men tend to be lousy letter writers or are only interested in sports and beer.

When I wrote that first letter to Diane, her address was a flat in Bethnal Green in East London. This, I would learn, was not her flat but a friend's who was letting her stay there while she looked for a new flat of her own. Diane always maintained that she was staying with a woman named Jean but I eventually deduced she was actually there with Jean's older son Barry. The relationship seemed rather casual but he apparently told Diane that all this letter writing was a waste of time. Luckily, she did not listen to him. She always said that she felt something special in my first letter – I think the tone as much as the content – and she wrote a very lovely letter in reply.

Dear David

Firstly, I would like to thank you for your delightful letter which I received on Friday and have only just found a little time to reply – after a very hectic but enjoyable weekend. Fortunately (or unfortunately), my writing is rather indecipherable too, and being a secretary I have access to that most convenient of machines, electric typewriter. I always find anyway that when writing a letter of this type that my mind flows faster than my hand so consequently am inclined to shorten things merely for the sake of speed.

My goodness, how to start about myself – I suppose I should tell you my age – which is 32 - my marital status divorced (thank goodness) and my interests varied. I am a legal secretary and have had quite a few jobs all to do with commercial business.

My main interest is music, from Bach to Aamon Duull, which if you don't know is a great German group who started up in the sixties and there are not many people who know who I am talking about when I mention them. I also adore science-fiction, especially the old black and white films. I very much enjoy seeing old movies with James Dean, James Cagney, Humphrey Bogart etc. A couple of years back I attended a science-fiction convention in Holland at one of the big hotels in Rotterdam, where for three whole days we all devoured films, books, food and drink. A very, very good time.

I also like to travel and have spent many happy vacations in France which is a country I have a distinct penchant for, mainly for the sun (I am a sun-lover, being an Arian), the good food and wine. I do have a desire to visit Nepal but the nearest I have approached is Morocco some four years ago. But I still have my hopes to reaching that country.

I was pleased to read that you liked the Goons, Spike Milligan is one of my favourite comedians – as was Peter Sellers. His passing was a great tragedy to the English profession and I shall always remember his Inspector Clouseau character with great affection.

I am living in the middle of London at the moment as you can see from my address and so I am able to go to all the rock concerts with ease, but I am hoping to move soon to a few miles further out of the city for a little peace and quiet, but will still be able to commute with not much difficulty. By the way, have you heard of Douglas Adams? (I couldn't find the question mark – I must have had a good time last night!)

To get back to Douglas Adams – he wrote a radio play a while back called "The Hitchhiker's Guide to the Galaxy" – which was an instant hit which was then put on the stage at the London Rainbow Theatre and then put on our television screens as a six-week series. The books, tapes, and records were also released and I have the books and records, but unfortunately not possessing a tape deck at the moment I cannot get the tapes.

Well, I'm afraid I don't know what more to say at this juncture – if I carry on I shall only bore you to tears, so I look forward to hearing from you – if you are inclined and please let me know if there is anything you would like to know about, any questions on any subject and I shall do my doubtful best to entertain you.

Do take great care, it's another day tomorrow,

Enjoy it!

Diane

I do not know what expectations I may have had when I decided to try being a pen friend but Diane's letter exceeded all of them. We both agreed that something clicked from those very first letters but neither of us quite knew what that something was or what it might become. It had taken about two weeks for Diane's reply to reach me – such was the pace of international snail mail, even by air – so I wasted no time in writing to her again. We wrote regularly and faithfully and felt a quiet little thrill every time an air mail envelope arrived.

An interesting aspect of our correspondence was that we did not exchange photographs right away. That must seem unthinkable in this age of the internet and selfies but it did not bother us, at least not immediately. In Diane's case, it was probably because of shyness and a lack of available photos. I think sending a photo simply did not occur to me at first. I do not know who initiated the eventual exchange or which photo I chose to reveal myself. The first picture I got of Diane was a little one from a photo booth. I thought she looked nicely appealing and conformed to my conception of an English secretary. I can still close my eyes and see that picture which is just as well as it disappeared over the years. Diane grew to hate the picture ("it's awful" she said) but I am not making any accussations.

It is amazing how many letters and cards we exchanged and all of them have been carefully preserved. If I put all of them in a book the resulting size would resemble *War and Peace.*

Of course, Diane and I did not write to one another exclusively. I had been given four other names and addresses while the pen friend club continued to send out Diane's details to other prospective correspondents. My other pen friends eventually fizzled out – three of them almost immediately. But I did acquire another pen friend from a different source – a girl named Nora in Northern Ireland with whom I have shared a different kind of correspondence with ever since although lately hard copy letters have turned into emails. We have shared lots of ups and downs and become good friends. Even Diane developed a certain affection for her.

Diane, however, was seemingly more ruthless with other possible pen friends, most of whom never got a reply. When I visited Diane for the first time, she picked up her post on our way out one day and saw yet another missive from an unknown person. She glanced at it briefly then stuffed it into a rubbish bin as we made our way up the street. But I later found out I was not the only one Diane has responded to favourably.

The lucky fellow was an older Jewish businessman from New York named Herbert who made regular trips to London. He invited Diane to spend a weekend with him at one of the best hotels. They had fancy meals, did some sightseeing and had a generally good time. Herbert was quite taken with Diane and suggested making their meetings a regular event, perhaps even setting her up in a new flat. Surprisingly, Diane's mother said she should at least consider the proposal but, even though Diane kind of liked Herbert, she decided that one weekend with him was enough.

I sort of heard about this in a letter Diane wrote a few days later in which she talked about her wonderful weekend. She wrote things like "On Saturday, we had quite a delightful trip on the river up to Greenwich. Then on Sunday went to one of my favourite art galleries, the Tate" without ever explaining who the "we" were. She told me about it years later and recounted the episode matter-of-factly and without guilt, not that she had anything to feel guilty about. After all, I was still married at the time and she was a free agent. Diane laughingly confided that Herbert told her she had a "tight little ass" which she considered a hilarious compliment.

While Herbert was apparently nothing more than a memorable weekend in August, I thought it was interesting that Diane saved the half dozen or so letters from him. They were hardly love letters and mostly were about his business travels to places like Guyana, Jakarta and Hong Kong. His later letters also made occasional references to her body and making love but nothing specific or explicit. I would love to know what Diane wrote to him, especially as she was writing to me quite frequently at the time. Whatever she said, the correspondence was over by November. I can only wonder if Herbert ever contacted any other women on his Harmony list. My only disappointment was that I was not Diane's first American.

In the meantime, Diane and I continued to write letters and even send little gifts to one another. That summer, she found a nice one bedroom flat in Ilford that she liked and left Bethnal Green for good. Oddly, she seldom ever mentioned Jean or Barry again. Diane had an upstairs flat in a large house that had just been converted into four flats. Her mother came to stay with her and to help her fix up the new place. The two of them worked hard even though they were constantly reduced to fits of giggles in the process. Diane's dark days seemed to finally be behind her.

As our friendship progressed, Diane and I wrote to each other about all sorts of things from very serious (my marriage, her diabetes) to very silly. In one letter, I mentioned my involvement with belly dancing and enclosed one of the belly dance business cards. Of course, the card contained my home telephone number and that was a temptation Diane could not possibly resist.

Diane in her new flat

I came home from work one day to see that there were a couple of messages on the answering machine. The first was from a confused female with a strange accent who kept saying "Hello…hello…is anybody there…am I through to Baltimore? Hello!" before hanging up. This was followed by a second message in which the same voice, now much calmer, said that it was Diane and that she would try ringing later on in the hopes I would be home. There were very obvious office noises in the background. She finished by saying: "I hate these answering machines."

Diane did indeed ring later for what was to be the first of many long and expensive but wonderful long distance chats. We were no longer just pen friends although this did not affect the quantity of our letter writing. I found the two messages on the answering machine so endearing that I made a copy of them on cassette. I still have it. Now, whenever I want to, I can listen to the time I first heard Diane's voice.

It was obvious that Diane and I were becoming more than just simple pen friends. Even my wife Jackie realised it but she seemed ambivalent about it probably because it eased whatever sense of guilt she may have had over her own extra-curricular activities. I started to make cassette tapes to send to Diane filled with music, little creative touches, a long stretches of simply talking to her. Sometimes Diane let her mother listen to them, until they became more personal.

During one of our phone calls, the subject of Diane's flat came up. There was a slight pause, then Diane said in a quiet voice: "If you ever come to London, you can stay with me." I don't know if she meant it or was joking or just being polite but I took it as an invitation and immediately began researching how to get from Baltimore to London and badgering my boss to give me enough time off to make a trip to England worthwhile. It almost seemed as though dreams really could come true.

==

FOUR – THE FIRST TIME

By December, I had acquired my passport and booked a flight to London. The trip would not be until March and the anticipation was immense. If anything, the frequency of letters and phone calls to and from Diane increased. Like me, she had arranged to take three weeks off from work. I remember my boss asking me if Jackie and Nick were looking forward to going to England and the surprised look on his face when I casually replied: "Oh, they're not going."

The only direct flight from Baltimore to London in those days was on the small, no-frills World Airways who made the trip once a week. It was an overnight flight that was scheduled to land around 7am. To save Diane travelling all the way to Gatwick Airport, we had arranged to meet at the much smaller Victoria Coach Station. Because I was nervous about using British Rail on my own, I decided to make the connection on a Green Line coach which look longer but was more scenic.

Jackie drove me to BWI – which I still referred to by its much nicer former name of Friendship Airport. When I checked in, I was informed the flight would be delayed by at least an hour. My first thought was that Diane would have no way of knowing this so I asked Jackie, when she got home, to give Diane a quick call to tell her. Of course, she never did. While I waited, I wandered into the tiny duty free shop and thought it would be nice to buy a carton of American cigarettes for Diane.

It was a long flight but I doubt that I slept very much. The sun was shining when we landed and, despite what I had heard about the British weather, it was a pleasant spring day. I have no memory of passport control or baggage claim but I do know I changed a fairly large amount of cash with a very nice lady who pointed me in the direction of the Green Line pickup point. As luck would have it, I just missed a coach and would have to wait half an hour for the next one.

Meanwhile, Diane was a bundle of nerves and impatience at Victoria Coach Station where she smoked one cigarette after another and occasionally chatted with a sympathetic security guard. I was still on the coach when I first saw Diane and I recognised her immediately. As I got off, she threw her arms around me with both affection and relief. We both seemed to talk at the same time and I have no idea what we said in those first moments together. I paused only to collect my rather heavy suitcase – they did not have ones with wheels in those days – then followed Diane to the taxi rank for the cross town ride to Liverpool Street Station.

We passed a lot of famous landmarks, including Big Ben which was not as big as I thought it might be, but mostly our eyes were on each other with only brief silences in between some fairly excited chatter. At Liverpool Street, I waited while Diane bought me a ticket then I followed her onto the train that would take us to Ilford. My first experience of British Rail was mostly confusion especially when I saw that the second station on our route was named Maryland. I struggled with my case up the stairs at Ilford Station and we emerged into beautiful downtown Ilford.

The thing I vividly recall about Ilford as we came out of the station was the sight of so much rubbish being blown about by a gentle breeze. As we walked towards Diane's flat, there was less rubbish but frequent bits of dog poo on the pavement. I suddenly remembered a friend of my father's, who had been stationed in England during the war, once saying: "The English are a dirty people." At the time, I thought he must be wrong. It certainly did not look like this in the movies.

I was relieved that Northbrook Road looked much nicer in comparison. It was a gently curving street with well-kept Edwardian houses, many of which had been converted into flats. It suddenly looked very English but my main thought was how happy I would be to finally put down my suitcase. Diane seemed to talk more than I did and I became aware that she was even more nervous than I was.

When we finally arrived at Number 46, I had one more flight of stairs to haul my case up to Flat D. We came into Diane's little flat down a short hallway that went past a bathroom and a bedroom and led to the sitting room with a doorway to the bijou kitchen beside it. The place was simple but utterly charming and there was little doubt that the occupant was female. Diane told me to sit on the sofa while she made some coffee. The two-seater sofa could be opened up into a bed and I assumed that was where I would be spending the night.

Diane gave me a cup of milky coffee and a couple of digestive biscuits which were the first things I had eaten since the night before. I should have been tired with jet lag but I was too excited for that. Instead of joining me on the sofa, Diane took her coffee to a small table by the window and picked up the telephone. She was soon in a very animated conversation with her mother. To my horror, she carried the phone over to me and with a big smile said: "Say hello to Mum." I have seldom had good experiences with girls' mothers so it was an awkward, polite and mercifully brief conversation.

After Diane had hung up the phone. She finished her coffee and once again failed to sit beside me on the sofa. Instead, she excused herself while she went into the bedroom to change, leaving me alone with more thoughts than I could reasonably handle. Up until now, Diane had been wearing a rather smart suit that she had borrowed from her sister. When she came out of the bedroom she looked much more relaxed – and more attractive – in jeans and a very loose, gold-coloured sweater. She finally sat next to me and lit a cigarette, offering me one which I was to learn was a polite English custom. It was not yet noon on the first day of my three weeks with Diane.

I am sure we were both feeling nervous but our conversation did not reflect that. Diane told me later that she had been worried I would not like her when I actually met her. She actually had visions of me getting back on the coach and going back to Gatwick to return home. I had similar fears but all those thoughts almost instantly disappeared. We had liked each other in our letters and phone calls – now that we were physically together, we liked each other even more. I would love to know what was going through Diane's mind at that moment.

Our coffee finished, Diane picked up the cups and took them into the kitchen. I followed her and we ended up facing one another in the opening between the kitchen and the sitting room. For one of those long magical moments that supposedly only happen in movies, we looked at each other. And then we kissed. It was quite passionate for a first kiss and our embrace seemed to indicate that we did not want it to end. My most vivid memory of that moment was slipping my hand under the back of Diane's sweater, being delighted that she was not wearing a bra, and feeling the sensation of a body that felt like no other in my experience. Eventually the kiss ended and Diane took my hand and led me into her bedroom.

It will be my policy in relating the story of my relationship with Diane to pass over such scenes when taste and decorum and the censor dictates. Suffice to say that I would not be spending my nights on the sofa-bed.

The most embarrassing moment of that first visit – one that might have doomed any chance of romance between less enlightened lovers – was Diane's unconcealed mirth when she first saw my all- American, all-white Fruit of the Loom underpants which I had thoughtlessly worn when not knowing what might happen when we actually met. The garment provided a running joke and one of the first things I did on my return to Baltimore was to purchase a more colourful (and hopefully sexier) selection of briefs.

Everything eventually caught up with me and I apparently crashed out for the rest of the afternoon. Diane woke me in time for supper. I had worried about what kind of meals I would encounter in England but the aroma coming from the kitchen was more than promising. Diane had cooked me a pork chop – much thicker than the ones in the States – and had made some chips. These were real chips she had made herself from real potatoes, not frozen ones. I was amazed that such things were possible. She also produced a two litre bottle of Pepsi because she knew it was my favorite drink although, like most British people at the time, she served it at room temperature. All things considered, my first meal with Diane was a delightful and tasty experience. But I would soon realise that working girl Diane was operating on a very tight budget.

The next morning I awoke refreshed and very happy that the preceding day had not been a dream. Diane was in a very bubbly mood that I would learn was normal. She decided to give me a gradual introduction to England by taking me on an extended wander around Ilford, in particular down the High Road. Now that I was over any lingering jet lag, Ilford looked much better (and cleaner) than my initial impression. As we strolled past the various shops along the High Road and the adjacent Cranbrook Road, I began to realise that it reminded me of the way the Highlandtown area of Baltimore looked twenty-five years before. In fact, the feeling of going slightly back in time was a recurring one that was interrupted only by the more recent fashions and advertising posters.

Diane had a practical reason for wanting to go out. Because her fridge was rather small as was her kitchen storage space, she usually needed to go shopping every two or three days. But we did not go to a supermarket – not that there was one in sight. Instead we made a series of visits to a butcher, a greengrocer, a baker and even a newsagent. It all seemed amazingly quaint and I was a good guest by insisting on paying for all the purchases. After all, Diane had saved me a hotel bill and I had lots of English money in my pocket.

Beautiful downtown Ilford

The next day was Saturday and Diane had bought a pair of tickets to see the latest Tom Stoppard play *The Real Thing* at the Strand Theatre in London's famous West End. It was an experience I was really looking forward to. But Saturday did not begin well.

Because she had to do her insulin injection, Diane was usually an early riser. But that day I awoke to find her still in bed. When I tried to rouse her, I got no response. At the time, I knew very little about diabetes but something in the back of my head reminded me of hearing about hypos when someone's blood sugar goes so low that they become unconscious. I tried not to panic and decided to ring Diane's mother for advice. When I told her what was happening, her response was: "Oh, no, not again!" She told me to try and get something sweet into Diane, preferably sugar. I found a small canister of sugar in the kitchen, grabbed a spoon, cradled the limp and naked Diane in my arms, and proceeded to try to feed her some sugar. There was sugar everywhere and I could not be sure how much of it Diane was actually absorbing.

My attempts to revive Diane were constantly interrupted by phone calls from her mother who wanted to know what was happening. As the phone was in the sitting room, this meant I kept running back and forth. During the third call, I reported that little if any progress was being made. At this point, Annie was clearly as worried as I was and said I should ring for an ambulance.

Ringing 999 was not exactly the sort of experience I was hoping for when I came to England. I told the operator what was happening and gave the address. Then I went back to try to force some more sugar into Diane. Some of it had actually made it into her system because she was beginning to wake up by the time the ambulance arrived. But she was still confused and incoherent so the paramedics decided to wrap her up and take her to hospital. While they were moving her, I quickly got dressed and rushed to join them. In my haste and stupidity, I never thought to bring any of Diane's things.

We went to King George Hospital on Eastern Avenue (which has since been torn down and relocated farther away). Diane was taken to the emergency room while I found an uncomfortable seat in a rather dreary waiting room. This was my introduction to the famous National Health Service I had heard so much about.

Eventually, a nurse came out to tell me that Diane was recovered and ready to go home. The problem was that the only thing she was wearing was a hospital blanket. I said I would sort something out despite having no idea how to do that. The nurse pointed in the direction of a pay phone that had several business cards for minicab firms pinned next to it. With no previous experience of either of these things, I somehow managed to get through to a minicab company who said that a car would soon be outside near the door to the emergency room.

At the time, I was not sure what a minicab was so I was a bit surprised when an ordinary car pulled up in front of me and the driver asked: "Are you David?" I got into the car and briefly explained that I needed to go to my girlfriend's flat, get some clothes for her to take back to the hospital, then for the two of us to go back to the flat. When I told the driver our initial destination was Northbrook Road he asked: "Where's that?" I tried to explain that I had only been in the country a couple of days and was in no position to give directions. After a couple of minutes, I suggested that if he could find his way to Ilford Station I could direct him from there.

After what must have been a very roundabout route, we made it to the flat. I asked the driver to wait while I rushed inside. Not wanting to use a plastic bag, I chucked out the contents of my flight bag and threw in the clothes that Diane had been wearing the night before. As I was leaving the flat, the phone rang and I decided to ignore it. Back at the hospital, I was shown to a closed off cubicle where Diane was waiting very unhappily – the first time I ever saw her like that. She quickly got into her clothes and, after bemoaning the lack of a hair brush and her glasses, followed me to the waiting car.

By this time the bemused driver had a better idea of where to go and we were soon back at the flat. The ride had passed in silence. Diane hurried inside leaving me to settle up with the driver. Minicabs do not have meters but charge according to distance. When I asked what the fare was, the driver merely shrugged. I gave him a ten pound note which seemed to make him more than happy. When I got back into the flat, I could hear Diane on the phone talking to her mother ("You'll never see him again" was the verdict Diane reported to me years later. I went first to the bathroom then collapsed onto the bed.

When Diane came in to lie beside me, she was looking very sheepish. "Sorry about that," she mumbled. "Well," I said, perhaps selfishly and perhaps trying to change the subject, "so much for the theatre tonight." Diane suddenly seemed much brighter. "Oh, no," she said, "I'll be fine by then." And, amazingly, she was.

I, of course, had known that Diane was diabetic but the implications of that were not apparent until that morning. I would become something of an expert over the years and the ways of testing blood sugar levels and dealing with hypos would improve considerably. In the end, that morning had probably been more traumatic for me than for her although Diane had to clear up all the sugar that seemed to be all over the bedroom.

The play – with Roger Rees and Felicity Kendal – was wonderful. It had been a rush to get there on time so afterwards Diane suggested that we go for a stroll. Except for the taxi ride from Victoria to Liverpool Street this was my first experience of being out on the streets of London. Even so, I was initially apprehensive. In America, wandering around a big city late at night was considered dangerous but Diane assured me that was not the case in London. So we strolled arm in arm down the Strand, around Trafalgar Square and on to Pall Mall with me still peering over my shoulder at the sound of other footsteps.

Over the next three weeks we alternated busy days in London with more leisurely ones in Ilford. I was, of course, excited to finally be in London, a place I had dreamed about for years, so there was a certain amount of being a typical tourist. We went to places like St. Paul's Cathedral and the Tower of London and I was surprised to learn that Diane had never been there even though she had lived all her life in London. Maybe she was simply too busy. Sometimes we spent the day in Ilford and went to see a play in the West End in the evening. Other times we just mooched or wandered around. On Good Friday, we ignored the nonstop rain and spent most of the day in bed. The important thing was we were together.

On good days, we could get from Ilford to Liverpool Street in about fifteen minutes on the train. But on most days, we got off at Stratford to change to the Central Line of the Underground which ran all across London and interchanged with the other lines. At first I was a bit unsure about this move since the only similar system I was aware of was the New York subway which had a terrible reputation at the time. Diane laughed off my hesitation and insisted the London Underground was nothing like that. I soon began to appreciate the "tube" and its relative convenience. Among other things, it was a great place for people watching.

Even though this was 1983, the legacy of the Seventies was still apparent. As we wandered around town, we encountered hippies and punks and girls with wild hair and too much makeup co-existing with City gents in bowler hats, Cockney geezers and a somewhat dowdy older generation. In particular, I was fascinated by the girls of London who all seemed to be much thinner than their counterparts in America (sadly, this is no longer true). Apparently, some of this interest was returned. More than once when passing an attractive young thing, Diane would suddenly grasp my arm tightly and say "he's mine" which did my ego no end of good.

One day our wanders took us to Covent Garden, a place I had heard much about and even seen glimpses of in films. The old market had gone and was replaced by trendy (and pricey) little shops and cafes. But I was more interested in the Opera House (this was, of course, before it was re-modelled). We went into the lobby and looked over the listings of upcoming events. My attention was drawn to a performance by the Royal Ballet of a mixed program of three short ballets. I had often seen various ballet companies at the Kennedy Center but Diane, who had a lifelong love of dance, had never been to one. A quick check at the box office revealed there were two good seats in the balcony available. Whether it was for that night or a couple of nights later, I cannot remember but I promptly bought the tickets.

Just seeing the inside of the Opera House and climbing the great staircase was a treat in itself. The seats provided an excellent view of the stage. The first ballet on the program was actually *The Kingdom of the Shades,* taken from *La Bayadère.* It began with a long line of thirty-two dancers in glittering white costumes- the "shades" or ghosts - gracefully twirling their way down a long incline and gradually filling the stage which prompted Diane to whisper: "It's so beautiful!" I will never forget the look on her face. She was like a child on Christmas morning with a transfixed expression of wonder and delight. For a moment, I thought she was going to cry.

I am not sure what Diane thought about the second offering, a rather modernistic version of *The Prodigal Son* with choreography by George Balanchine but the final ballet was the stylish *La Fin du Jour* which featured elegant prima ballerina Merle Park and the exquisite Marguerite Porter who had also been in *La Bayadère.* Diane loved the entire experience and seemed almost to be dancing herself on our way back to the flat.

There was dancing of a different sort on another night. Diane's best friend at work was a fellow secretary named Lorraine who was a couple of years older and quite different. She was a warm-hearted extrovert who had taken Diane under her wing. She was also the most talkative person I ever met and reminded me of an old Groucho Marx line – you must have been vaccinated with a phonograph needle. She was in a relationship with a little chap named Ron – "my bit of rough" Lorraine called him – who worked at Truman's Brewery in Bethnal Green. The brewery was having a kind of disco on the premises one night and Lorraine and Ron decided that Diane and I should go along with them.

I was definitely seeing parts of London that tourists never see. The disco, which was really just a big party, was a boisterous affair in which the brewery's product flowed like water. I think Ron was slightly miffed when I said that I no longer drank alcohol and Diane preferred to have a scotch. I was definitely in the midst of Cockney London. I was also aware that Lorraine was carefully checking me out. As for the dancing, I think Diane and I had a little bop together but most of the evening remains fairly cloudy in my memory.

Our best times together were in the flat, especially when Diane was a trifle tipsy. One evening we sat on the floor with our backs against the sofa and were helpless with laughter as we listened to a cassette of Spike Milligan reading his novel *Puckoon.* We then put on some music and in an untypically reckless moment, I began to bounce my bottom along with the beat. Diane looked at me with disbelief then burst into the most raucous laughter I had ever heard. She said that "dancing my bum" was the funniest thing she had ever seen which only encouraged me. She went on to say: "It's not just the dancing of your bum that's so funny, it's the silly look on your face while you're doing it." For many years afterwards, Diane would frequently ask me to dance my bum to brighten up a particular moment.

A short walk from Diane's flat was Valentine Park which seemed to be a favourite place of hers. She took me there on a warm and sunny Sunday afternoon and I found it not only green and peaceful but also very English. There were gently sloping open areas fringed by shady wooded ones with footpaths going in all directions. A cricket match was in progress on the other side of a small boating lake and we also passed by a bowling green. There were plenty of benches and a small café. It was an oasis of calm and it did not take me long to totally relax and realise why Diane loved it so much.

On our way to the park, Diane suggested that we buy some shelled peanuts – which she always called "monkey nuts" - to feed to the squirrels. My experience with squirrels in Baltimore was that they were afraid of humans and would run away and scamper up the nearest tree. Diane assured me that English squirrels were different and would take the peanuts from our hands.

As we walked along a shady path, a squirrel suddenly appeared in front of us. He sat on his hind legs and looked at us both curiously and hopefully. Then he saw that I had some peanuts in my hand. Before I could bend down to offer him one, the frisky rodent was climbing up my leg. I must have jumped because the squirrel was soon back on the ground and surrounded by fallen peanuts. Diane thought the entire episode was hilarious. It was my introduction to British wildlife.

A quiet corner of Valentine Park

As the days passed by, I discovered more aspects of Diane's unique personality. She had a tendency at times to be somewhat hyper-active and to do things in a rush as though she was running out of time. This rush sometimes led to minor accidents but she seemed to need to be doing things all the time. She used to say to me: "Don't ever let me be bored". I assumed, rightly, that she was like this at work where she apparently existed on coffee and cigarettes and seldom took a lunch break. Diane had a compulsion to be helpful and was unable to say "no" when it came to assistance or extra work. I think the constant surge of adrenalin kept hypos at bay although the energy often faded by the time she returned home. But in our three weeks together she found it easier to relax and be relatively calmer – and endlessly endearing.

In the middle of our three weeks together was Diane's thirty-third birthday and we had planned long before to have a party to mark the occasion. It would not be a big party but a good opportunity for me to meet some of her friends – and her parents.

FIVE – PARTY AND PARTING

The party was on a Saturday so we did the shopping for it on Friday. There was a token supermarket in Ilford at the time – a compact Sainsbury's that was almost hidden in a corner of a small square just off the High Road a little farther down than we usually ventured. It was quite modest by American standards by it stocked just about everything we needed, including alcohol. As we roamed up and down the narrow aisles, throwing all manner of goodies into the shopping trolley, Diane seemed more concerned than happy. She later told me that she was mentally adding up the cost and wondering how many hours of overtime she would have to work to pay for it. Why she thought I was going to let her pay I can only attribute to her paying all the bills in her previous relationships. So she was very relieved when I whipped out one of my fifty pound notes at the till from which I got little change.

It seemed a long walk back to the flat with the handles of the heavy plastic carrier bags nearly cutting into our hands. Once inside the kitchen, Diane took charge of organising the purchases and told me to relax. Instead I went on a little solo foray back down the High Road in search of a suitable card and present for her birthday which was actually on Sunday. It was easy enough to find an amusing card but I had no idea what to do for a present. I prowled back and forth gazing into shop windows in search of inspiration and finally decided on a small but elegant carriage clock which I thought would look right at home in Diane's flat.

The reason we did the shopping on Friday was that Diane's parents were driving up from Hampshire on Saturday, not just for the party that evening but to spend the day with us – and to meet me. My track record with the families of girlfriends was not good – Jackie's family absolutely hated me – so I was jittery to say the least. Diane kept telling me not to worry but I think even she was unsure about the impending reaction.

Annie and Ron arrived in time for lunch. The introductions were not as awkward as I had feared. Annie was bright and animated, very much like her daughter, and their closeness was instantly apparent. Ron, on the other hand, was fairly quiet – the result, no doubt, of having lived for so long with three women. We shook hands firmly and he gave me a friendly smile before his expression returned to one worthy of Buster Keaton. Diane immediately suggested that we all have fish and chips – a treat she had introduced me to several days earlier when I was assured that vinegar was optional. What I did not realise was that Diane and Annie would be going to the nearby chippie, leaving me alone in the flat with Ron.

Diane's father was not dour or glum, he was simply very quiet. A couple of attempts at conversation were not successful. I think we both felt that the only thing we had in common was Diane – that and both being uncomfortable with strangers. The time passed mostly in silence and I could not believe how long it was taking to fetch some fish and chips. If I was told then what good friends Ron and I would ultimately become, I would not have believed it.

The overall mood was much more relaxed as the four of us devoured our cod and greasy chips. I enjoyed this very English meal despite the heavy aroma of vinegar in the air. Diane and her mother seemed to always be laughing and even Ron joined in the general merriment. Diane constantly gave me little glances as if to say I was doing all right. The two women then proceeded to do most of the party preparations while Ron settled in front of Diane's little television to watch some very English sport like cricket or snooker which I did not understand.

The other three flats in Diane's house were inhabited by single males but only one of them, Martin, who had the other upstairs flat and seemed to get on very well with Diane, was invited. My memory is unsure whether Lorraine, who also lived in Ilford at the time, came but if she did it was on her own. The rest of the guests were three couples Diane knew from her Gerry days.

A later picture of Diane and her parents –
I don't know why I didn't take more photos at the time.

Although I am not always good with names and faces, it was easy to tell these couples apart. There was the slightly hippyish Peter and Hilary who had accompanied Diane and Gerry on their infamous odyssey; the well-groomed Martin and his gorgeous wife Maria, and a haystack of a long-haired, big-bearded chap named Trevor and his pixie of a girlfriend Penny. While the beer and wine (and properly chilled Pepsi) flowed freely, it was safe to assume that Trevor was just a tad high on something else.

I was amazed at how well Diane's parents interacted with this motley assortment. Even Ron came to life and frequently laughed, usually at something Trevor had said or done. The parents sat by the table in the window while the rest of us either moved around or stretched out on the floor. I was getting a lot of attention including being asked for the sixteenth time: "What do you think of England?" Peter seemed surprised that I liked a lot of English bands such as the Kinks and Roxy Music. Martin (the one with Maria not the next door neighbour) told me that he liked America and that he and Maria had been married in San Francisco. Trevor told me at length about a comedy show called *The Young Ones* and even acted out bits of it. The girls, on the other hand, mostly just looked at me and smiled. Diane appeared pleased at how well things were going but I could not shake the feeling that her old friends were comparing me to Gerry whose name was never mentioned.

In the middle of the party, the phone rang and Diane answered it with the cheerful voice that came with scotch. She giggled slightly then called out across the room: "David, it's your wife!" As I made my way to the phone, I heard Annie murmuring "How embarrassing" but everyone else seemed to think it was quite funny. I had told Jackie in advance that we would be having this party and she had obviously decided to ring just to be a nuisance. The conversation was brief and mostly in words of one syllable. I was more angry than embarrassed and decided to retreat into the bedroom to calm down.

I was quickly followed by the petite and pretty Penny who decided that I needed consolation. We were soon joined by Diane who wanted me to come back to the party. After Penny left, Diane told me that the sweet little pixie had a reputation for trying to steal other girls' boyfriends.

The party went on much as before until people started to leave. Finally it was just Diane, her parents and me. Despite it being a long drive and a late hour, Annie and Ron planned to return to Hampshire that night and wanted to know if we wanted to go with them. Diane seemed to be of two minds but, even though the prospect of seeing the English countryside was intriguing, there was still more of London that I wanted to experience. So we said goodnight and I wondered what Diane's parents talked about on the long drive home.

The next day was Diane's birthday and we spent it together quietly and very happily. I could not help reflecting that on the same day the previous year neither of us was aware the other existed. So much can happen in a year. We seemed to be proof of the old adage that life is full of surprises. I cannot imagine having a more wonderful surprise than finding Diane.

I have to admit that Diane was full of good ideas during my stay. One of these was to go to the local theatre in Ilford – the Kenneth More Theatre – to see a production of *The Rocky Horror Show* whose mixture of comedy and science fiction appealed to her very much. I was normally not a big fan of amateur productions but I certainly was not going to refuse. As it turned out, it was a very enjoyable show well suited to the small theatre and acted with great enthusiasm by the cast. The only downside was that the evening came near the end of my three week visit.

The fact that all good things must come to an end is seldom good. The date of my departure was rapidly approaching and neither of us wanted to acknowledge it. When we did it was in practical terms rather than emotional ones. The unspoken thought was whether we would ever see each other again. During one long late night conversation when Diane had a bit more scotch than usual she said to me with a serious expression I had not seen before: "You have to decide what you want" and I knew she was right. We had packed a lot into three weeks and nearly all of it had been nothing but fun. But now we both wondered if it had just been a fling or the beginning of something more.

For some reason Diane decided she wanted to come to Gatwick Airport to see me off rather than saying goodbye in London or even at the flat. Airports are really not very nice places – they are big and noisy and crowded with people in a hurry. The check-in was relatively easy and once I had got rid of my big suitcase it was more comfortable for us to move around, even with Diane clinging to my arm. I tried not to keep looking at clocks or my watch but we both knew the final moment was almost upon us. Diane, ever very emotional, was already becoming tearful.

We finally found ourselves by the gate through which only passengers with boarding passes could go. We stood there for a long time, embracing but not saying very much. Our moment was interrupted by a broadly smiling Japanese couple who approached Diane and used a kind of sign language to ask her to take their picture. They thrust a camera into her hands which Diane merely looked at it in confusion through increasing tears. Before I could intervene, the Japanese girl suddenly realised they had asked the wrong person, gently took back the camera and the couple melted into the surrounding throng of indifferent humanity.

Diane and I kissed and repeatedly tried to say goodbye. I told her I would ring when I got back to Baltimore. Then I did one of the hardest things I had ever done – I gave her one last kiss and quickly went through the gate. After a few steps, I turned to look back. Diane was still standing there, tears in full flood, looking like a very sad and tiny lost soul. I felt numb as I went through the rest of the pre-flight procedures.

Once I was out of sight, Diane ran through the airport to the train station, totally unaware of her surroundings or any attention she may have drawn. On the train to Victoria, she cried most of the way, half curled up by a window. At one point, an older businessman asked what was wrong and offered to help her but she essentially ignored him. It was really stupid of me to let Diane come to Gatwick and then have to make her way back to Ilford on her own.

My plane was only about a third full – not unusual for World Airways – so I had a window seat with no one beside me. It was another clear and beautiful spring day and as I looked down on England it really did look like a green and pleasant land. My recurring thought was "What am I doing?" although I knew I had no other option at that time. Diane had cried so much that I did not want her to see a single tear in my eyes. But there were some as the long flight began.

Flying from east to west is always an odd experience because you are travelling with the sun and the day seems endless. Thus I took off from London at 2:30pm and landed in Baltimore at 4:30pm. That is a different kind of jet lag especially when doing it for the first time.

Not surprisingly, Jackie was late in picking me up. I expected the mood on the drive back to the house to be somewhat strained but she was almost polite in asking me about my trip, possibly because our son was in the car. Once home, I began to unpack and gave Jackie and Nick the souvenirs and presents I had bought them. Then Jackie told me that she had plans for that evening, went upstairs to change and was soon gone. I spent some time with Nick before remembering that I had promised to ring Diane. I went to the bedroom, closed the door and made the call.

I vividly recall that the first thing Diane said to me was: "You've left me the Pope!" In all our West End shopping we had amassed a collection of colourful carrier bags and one of these featured a large portrait of John Paul II who had visited London a year or two earlier. As a joke, I had left this bag on display in the bedroom. It was good to hear her voice even if she sounded more subdued than normal. For the time being at least, our relationship would continue to be a long distance one – but with many happy memories to sustain it.

The immediate aftermath of those three wonderful weeks seemed to affect us differently. For me, the primary feature of my return to "normality" was probably confusion. Some things had changed while I had been away. To begin with, Jackie's attitude towards me was noticeably different. She was even more distant than before and she had developed a kind of smugness which I assumed was because she now felt she had something on me. At the same time, my place of work had moved to a new location. The lease on the records warehouse had expired at the end of March and, for whatever reason, was not renewed. So new premises were secured all the way on the other side of town and the move took place in my absence. This change came about suddenly after I had booked my flights and I refused to change my plans. The Head Babe was not pleased. (My boss called everyone "babe" because he was terrible at remembering names. Some of us privately referred to him as The Head Babe. I was amused to discover that Diane also had a habit of calling people "babe" – but in a much friendlier way.)

Meanwhile Diane – who had a habit of taking her moods to the extreme – was stricken with sudden loneliness. I never realised how she felt in those first days after my departure until recently when I came across something that she wrote at the time – her frequent therapy of putting thoughts on paper. She wrote:

I rang David Saturday 9 April. He did not seem too bad – just slightly distant in attitude. Rang him again Wednesday 13th. Very early this time as we are 6 hours apart. 6:30am. He said that his situation is unchanged – if anything is worse. At the moment realize there is no possibility of any life together as he is one of those who will just be content to be left alone and lead a life a ease. If not exactly happy – at least comfortable albeit somewhat strange. Hence now is the time to take more charge of my own life. Will ask that he assist in forming or composing an advert to place in one of those crazy mags. I would like to meet a man from America – about 35 – reasonable means – who will take me as I am. To love me without overpowering. I'm 33 and need to love and be loved. God I'm getting old. Is there any hope? Yes, dammit.

Going to Ivy Gibson Bureau on Saturday – just off Bond Street to see what there is to see. Being of a romantic frame of mind of course I hope for something – someone. Feel a bit ashamed really but at least I am doing something other than just sitting moping. That time is definitely at an end. I am fed up with living alone. Cannot take it much longer. Will no longer move within my own sphere as I have done for so long. I want someone who wants me and who will take me out in the old-fashioned sense of the word. Look after me etc. I want to look after them too. Whoever it is to be. I need a man in my life. David does not want me. Good I can accept and take that. He has not hurt me. I love him.

I can only think that I might have sounded distant to Diane because I was tired and depressed. My feelings for her certainly had not changed in any way that would cause her to have such thoughts. Luckily, the mood passed and the next few calls and letters reassured her that I did indeed love her very much.

Both my home and work situations had deteriorated and I found myself increasingly wishing I was back in Ilford. The long commute to the new warehouse quickly turned into a major hassle while Jackie and I were more like roommates than a married couple. I think even Nick, who was twelve by this time, could sense the tension. Even so, I continued to play the role of husband and father. I put together a music tape and acted as stage manager for a children's dance recital of which Nick was a less than enthusiastic participant. I even did several belly dance gigs with Jackie although she continued to do a number of "bellygrams". We also went to a few movies as a family. But I did not let anything interfere with my stream of letters and occasional phone calls to Diane.

Things were never going to be the same as they were before my trip to England. Diane seemed to feel much the same way and there were frequent moments of intimacy in our communication. But there were also times when I simply sat alone and thought about Diane's words: "You have to decide what you want." I decided I wanted Diane.

===

SIX – BACK AND FORTH

In slightly less than a year, what had started out as a relatively innocent communication between pen friends had turned into something much more. Neither Diane nor I had expected this to happen and we were not looking – at least not consciously – for a new relationship. Diane was still recovering from her previous traumatic relationship and certainly not looking for love but, at the same time, she was not the sort of person who fancied the prospect of living on her own for too long. Meanwhile I could not believe I was falling in love with a wonderful English girl. I may have dreamed about such a thing but I thought that was all it was – a dream. But now I was 35 and at a point where I either had to make a drastic change in my life or resign myself to staying in the same rut.

During our frequent phone calls, our discussions about the future gradually changed from "if" to "when and how". I wanted to act as soon as possible but Diane was more cautious. There were many things to be considered and sorted out, not least of which were my divorce and the legalities of settling in another country. We both did some research, some of which turned out to be misleading. We really could have done with the internet back then. I had never been a particularly impulsive person but I was becoming more and more inclined to act on this impulse.

One evening on the long drive home from work I told Jackie that I thought we should split up and that I wanted to go back to England. To my surprise, she took this quite calmly and agreed almost immediately. We both knew that our marriage was in permanent decline and she was happily involved with at least three other (married) men on a semi-regular basis. Her only disappointment was that she had always assumed she would be the one who left. My main feelings of guilt concerned our son but I told myself that he would be better off with a single parent rather than two who existed in a toxic atmosphere. It would also not be long before I announced my intention to quit my job after twelve years to a seemingly indifferent Head Babe.

Diane seemed quite surprise when I told her I had booked a flight to London in June. I could tell that her delight was mixed with apprehension – she found the prospect of making another commitment somewhat scary. But, based on our previous three weeks together, it was a gamble we were both willing to take.

As it turned out, the date for my flight was in the middle of a week when Jackie and Nick were on vacation with her family in the mountains of Western Maryland so I had the house to myself for a few days which gave me lots of time to think. I decided it was probably a good idea to tell my parents what was happening. They didn't want to discuss it on the phone so they came to the house where I tried to give them a brief summary of the circumstances and my intentions. They listened quietly and with no noticeable emotion but I knew they were not happy about the situation. In keeping with my role as black sheep, I was to be the first person in our family to get a divorce, although there were possibly a few others who should have. In the end, it was my parents who gave me a ride to the train station where we said our restrained goodbyes.

In an attempt to save money, I foolishly booked my flight with the then-popular People Express, a short-lived, low cost, no frills airline that made a weekly flight from Newark, New Jersey to London Gatwick. So I first had to travel by train from Baltimore to Newark. All things considered, the reduced fare was probably not worth it. The airline had a haphazard reservations system in which nothing was guaranteed until you actually booked in. As it was summer, the tiny terminal was full of backpackers trying to get a cheap flight. I heard one of them say: "If we can't get on the London flight, we'll get one to Florida." There had been media reports of wild parties on People Express but my flight was quiet. I managed to get some sleep but was woken up mid-flight so that I could pay my fare with a credit card.

As usual, it was an overnight flight so I arrived at Gatwick early on a Saturday morning. Even though Diane was not at work, we had decided not to meet in town. Instead I would make my own way to the flat since I was now familiar with the various transport in London. I must have looked like some sort of bedraggled refugee by the time I reached Northbrook Road but Diane greeted me with happy smiles, hugs and kisses. It was almost, but not quite, as if I had never left.

Things would be different this time. Diane would be going to work so I would be left to my own devices. Luckily I had a fair amount of cash left over from my previous trip to which I had managed to add some. This would help to keep us going for a while and I hoped to be able to find some sort of job. But in those first few hours, all practicalities were dismissed from our minds as we warmly resumed our loving relationship. To say that I felt a great sense of relief is an example of typical British understatement.

The following Monday, Diane had to go to what she called the "ghoul clinic" – a check-up clinic for diabetics at the Royal London Hospital in Whitechapel, former home of the Elephant Man in the heart of Jack the Ripper territory. Diane always seemed amused by my fascination with history but she gradually learned to appreciate it. Anyway, Diane's mother usually came up to London to accompany her on these occasions and this was no exception. We met her at Liverpool Street Station, had breakfast in a greasy spoon café and took the tube to Whitechapel. After the usual long NHS wait, Diane had a few basic tests and then an interview with a doctor. It all seemed harmless enough but Diane was relieved when it was over. We then had lunch at a Wimpy's across the street, went back to Liverpool Street where we said goodbye to Mum and made our way back to the peace and quiet of the flat.

After that we settled into what would become our usual routine. For some reason, the one bedroom flat seemed slightly smaller than before. I tried to stay out of Diane's way as she rushed about in the morning getting ready for work. Then I was on my own. There was not a lot to do in the flat. British television only consisted of four channels in those days and, except for the news, they were all uninspiring. I made myself useful by doing some shopping including preparing a fairly simple lunch. It was summer but British summers were much milder than the hot and humid ones in Baltimore. I remembered that someone had once described British summers as being six weeks of warm rain.

Diane was usually quite tired when she returned home, especially on the two nights a week when she worked extra hours for what she regarded as necessary overtime pay. She often told me all about her day and I grew familiar with her co-workers and bosses if only by name. Diane was always saying that "solicitors were a breed apart". She particularly liked to tell stories about her boss – a rising star in the firm named Nick Edgell – because he was so prim and proper and used military expressions such as "chop chop" and "double away" when giving orders. Diane and Edgell had a very good working relationship and she seemed to have a degree of affection for him. I used to tease her about having an affair with him, a thought that horrified her. It turned out that this legal eagle and I had been born on the exact same day – 11 March 1948 – which to my mind proved the silliness of astrology.

Part of my daily routine was to meet Diane after work outside Ilford Station. The station had a small side entrance that was only open during rush hours and provided a short cut back to the flat. I used to sit on a low wall facing this entrance and watch the commuters coming out from trains that ran at roughly ten minute intervals. I was never sure which train Diane was on but I did not mind waiting. It was a good place for people watching and I liked to invent little stories about some of the people and even invented nicknames for a few I saw regularly. When Diane eventually appeared, we were both very glad to see one another and walked together to the flat like a pair of lovers which, coincidentally, we were.

When I first met Diane, she had a kind of blemish about six inches across on the inside of one of her legs. She told me it was from a burn she had received several years earlier when riding on the back of a motorcycle in a short skirt. The mark was in the process of fading and it would be several more years before it completely disappeared. It was a reminder – not that I needed one – of the sort of free spirit she once was and would always, at least partly, remain. Diane was frequently rather wistful about her past but did not always want to talk about it.

I shall never forget a somewhat quirky nightdress that Diane had. It was more of an over-sized t-shirt that she had found in Petticoat Lane, one of her favourite shopping haunts. The shirt had thin multi-coloured stripes and on the front in very cheerful letters were the words: "Don't try to understand me, just love me." It was the best advice I ever had in my relationship with Diane. She wore that nightdress until it virtually fell apart and we both missed it. Years later, I searched the internet for a similar one but never found it.

It was about this time that I first met Diane's older sister Lynne who had come up from Hampshire for an overnight visit. It was difficult not to notice the differences in the two. Lynne was taller, pretty and full of self-confidence. She did not seem to be as outgoing as Diane or their mother. I would not go so far as to say she was cold but she definitely did not have the same degree of warmth as Diane and Annie. The relationship between the sisters was hard to determine as it always seemed to be changing. Diane had told me that Lynne had been very bossy when they were children – even calling Diane "stupid" at times – yet there seemed to be a close bond between them that alternately grew and diminished over the years but never completely disappeared. What Lynne thought about me was impossible to tell.

The purpose of Lynne's visit was not so much to see her sister but to have a discreet place to be with her current boyfriend, a good looking but penniless chap named Lawrence. Diane seemed happy enough to accommodate them (not for the first time) but the situation reminded me too much of my wife Jackie's behaviour. This probably affected my attitude towards Lynne. The sisters' mother apparently suspected something like this had been going on and for years afterward tried to get an admission out of Diane who always managed to avoid answering. Annie even asked me about it once but I simply feigned ignorance which was always an easy act for me.

On this occasion, Lynne and her companion had to make do with the sofa-bed. Previously, when Diane was living alone, the soft-hearted younger sister offered the couple her bed while she slept in the sitting room. Diane told me that one time she had got up to visit the loo during the night and afterwards, half asleep and out of habit, she went into the bedroom and started to get into the bed. Diane always slept naked in those days and Lawrence must have thought it was his lucky night. Diane suddenly realized her mistake and beat a hasty retreat to the sitting room. I cannot imagine why she never wanted to share this amusing anecdote with her mother.

One of my faults at that stage in my life was an apparent inability to let money burn a hole in my pocket. I felt that just because we were no longer on vacation was no reason for not going out occasionally. So I got us tickets to see *Look Back in Anger* at the Kenneth More Theatre which, unfortunately, Diane did not enjoy too much. To make up for that, I bought some tickets to see the Royal Ballet's new production of *Isadora.* I knew that Diane had always been fascinated with the dancer Isadora Duncan and had read her autobiography and seen a couple of films about her so I knew this was something she would want to see. Of course, she loved it and the success of that evening out prompted me to book seats for the Royal Shakespeare production of *Much Ado About Nothing* at the Barbican featuring Derek Jacobi, an actor we both had admired in *I, Claudius* on television. This led to several more nights out, both in London and at the Kenneth More. I was probably being frivolous but I felt it was worth it.

Unfortunately, interspersed with all this fun, Diane had a couple of really bad hypos that required an ambulance and a trip to the emergency room at King George Hospital. After the second of these, I was approached by the fearsome figure of a senior nurse who told me in no uncertain terms that this sort of behaviour was unacceptable and that I should be doing more to prevent it. No one had spoken to me like that since the nuns at my primary school and I could only nod helplessly in reply. Diane, as usual, was extremely apologetic afterwards and promised to exercise better control. But Diane, I was to find out, frequently lived on the edge. Luckily, I began to recognise early warning signs. We did not have handy tubes of glucose in those days so I had to try to bring Diane's sugar up as best I could. One thing that seemed to work was small chocolate chip cookies which she would munch slowly if I asked her very nicely. Even so, she could still be mischievous and refuse to eat a cookie if it did not have sufficient chocolate chips in it.

Into our little domestic scene we now introduced a cat. Diane's friend Lorraine had several cats that she was anxious to find homes for so we went over there to take our pick. Diane fell in love with a small grey tabby that was called Mum because it took a motherly interest in the other cats. Mum was gentle and very affectionate and it was an easy choice. Once in the flat, she easily got used to her new surroundings and decided that yes, she would let us take care of her.

They say that dogs have owners but cats have staff. That certainly seemed to be true with Mum as she became both a focal point and Diane's "baby".

One afternoon, Diane rang me from work in a somewhat agitated state. She had just seen her ex-husband Gerry. He knew where she worked and had loitered outside the building until he saw her. The encounter was brief – Diane was in a hurry – but Gerry was insistent that they talk. He had several times before tried to get back into her life but she always found the strength to resist. She said that finally saying "No" to Gerry was one of the hardest, but also one of the proudest, moments in her life. But Diane only had so much strength and finally agreed to talk to him – but not on her own. She invited him to come to the flat that evening. Now he knew her new address but they both knew I would be there.

Gerry arrived just before 9pm ("I'm certainly not having him to dinner" Diane had said). She met him at the door and led him upstairs to the flat where he and I both cast our first suspicious looks at each other. Gerry was just a month older than me but he looked like he was nearly ten years older. Diane and I sat on the small sofa – she only let go of my arm to light cigarettes – while Gerry sat facing us, trying to assess the situation. Whether he really wanted Diane back or merely wanted to borrow money, he soon realised he was getting nothing. I do not think the encounter lasted very long although it seemed endless. Diane remained seated when Gerry got up to leave.

I escorted Gerry downstairs to the front door. As I opened the door for him, he smiled at me and said: "Take good care of our girl." When I told that to Diane, she replied with some very unladylike language. That was the only time I ever saw Gerry. He turned up outside Diane's office building a couple of more times that year. The last time he wanted to borrow some money to buy his new twenty-one year old girlfriend a nice dress because they were both due to appear in court. Gerry more or less disappeared after that. Over the years Diane would think aloud every now and then: "I wonder what happened to Gerry" without really seeming to care. After finally meeting him in person, I still could not understand the attraction but he probably thought the same about me.

As my money was obviously not going to last forever I tried to find some sort of employment but ran into legal roadblocks. I had mistakenly believed that if I could get a job, a work permit would come with it. It turns out that so long as I had a visitor's stamp in my passport (good for six months) I was ineligible for any kind of work in the UK. For that I would need to be classified as a resident and the easiest way to do that was to marry a British citizen. But, of course, I was still married. Diane had been right – I should have sorted everything out before coming back.

With great reluctance, I booked a flight back to Baltimore at the end of August. At least this time we would only be saying *au revoir*. Diane went with me as far as Liverpool Street Station. From there, she went to work and I continued on to the airport. I do not remember much about the journey. Because I could not think of anyone else, I asked Jackie to pick me up at BWI. As always, she was late.

Jackie was adamant that I was not going to stay in the house, not even on an old army cot in the basement. We went to the house so that I could pick up a few things, including my typewriter, and while there I rang my parents, explained my new situation and asked if I could stay with them while I sorted things out. Going back to my parents' house – and to my old bedroom – seemed like a very low point in my existence.

I was lucky to find a job fairly quickly – again as a warehouse manager, this time for a very large family-owned department store. With little else to do, I threw myself into the work of re-organising the various storage areas and setting up procedures for stock control. It was a new position. I had originally applied to work in the book department but once the owner became aware of my experience he decided that I was just what he needed. It kept me busy but I still had plenty of time to write several letters a week to Diane and every once in a while treat myself to a phone call. She reported that for the first couple of days after I left, Mum the cat kept prowling around the flat looking for me.

Living with my parents was not exactly easy and it was virtually impossible to ever feel totally relaxed. We never really talked about anything serious but I sensed my life choices did not have their complete approval. Other members of my family were more obvious in their disapproval. Not only was I, a Catholic, going to divorce my wife (who they all seemed to like) but I was compounding the sin by taking up with a foreign Protestant.

The most telling moment came on Christmas Day which was usually celebrated in my parents' house with quiet formality. My siblings by now all lived in different places along the east coast so this time only my brother Bob and his family came to visit for the holiday. Bob had, at some point, changed from a fairly carefree individual into a religious nut and his stern-faced wife was little better. Still, the conversation around the dinner table was polite and innocuous. At one point – and I cannot remember what was being discussed – I started to say "One time Diane and I..." As soon as her name was mentioned, a frozen silence descended with my brother and his wife staring solemnly down at their plates. I resisted the urge to say anything else and simply left the table and spent the rest of the day in my room. I have not had any communication with my brother Bob or his wife since.

There is a rather interesting footnote to this. Some years later I found out that Bob's eldest daughter got divorced and then married a Jewish man. Even more, she now considers herself to be Jewish. I can only wonder how Pope Bob reacted to all of that.

At one point while we were apart, possibly in an effort to feel less lonely, Diane had decided to have another party with her old friends. She told me about it in advance and I resisted the temptation to ring on the night. It was probably just as well. No one turned up. I can only imagine how upset Diane must have been especially if she had made all her usual elaborate preparations. The mental image I had of her sitting alone in her flat that night was a very sad one.

What I really needed to do was to get my divorce. Although Jackie agreed not to contest the divorce, the only grounds she would accept were that of irreconcilable separation which required our being apart for at least twelve months. I did not want to wait that long so I enlisted a friend of mine Joe, who had once been the van driver for my warehouse and now owned a pizza shop, to swear that Jackie and I had been separated for a year. This minor bit of perjury was successful and the wheels were set in motion. After the hearing, I went back to work while Jackie and Joe retired to my former bedroom to celebrate something or other. By the end of March 1984, I was officially a free man and could begin to plot my return to England, hopefully this time for good.

I sent Diane a card, one of those cards with a nice picture on the front that was blank inside for personal messages. The only thing I wrote in it was: "Will you marry me?"

Diane was delighted about my divorce but oddly less enthusiastic about my plans to return, possibly in May. She wanted me to wait a bit longer so that things could be properly organised. Besides, she added, she was due to go on holiday with her parents to the south of France and she wanted to have a nice tan for the wedding. I was disappointed at any possible delay but decided it would give me a chance to earn some extra money as well as get my tax refunds.

It was later revealed that the reason for the delay was that Diane was suffering with kidney stones and did not know how long the treatment would take. She laughed out loud when an Asian doctor at the hospital told her: "We have defused the situation!" She had recovered in time for her holiday and had a great time in the sun. Her mother thoughtfully took a few pictures of Diane in her topless bikini and these were sent on to me in due course. How many girlfriends' mothers would do something like that?

I went ahead and booked a flight with good old World Airways for mid-July. When they returned from holiday, Diane & Co. set about organising things for the wedding which would take place in Hampshire. Apparently, because of my so-called special circumstances, a special licence was required for the marriage. This had to be applied for, in person, at least three weeks in advance of the ceremony which was booked at the registry office in the town of Ringwood for August 4. As it turned out, the last day to make this application was the day I would be arriving. So Diane informed me that she and her father would meet me at Gatwick and we would then drive to Hampshire in time to do the necessary paperwork.

I had only a few goodbyes to say before I left Baltimore. The hardest was to my son – the easiest to his mother. While I had been working, I gave a portion of my pay to Jackie for child support (there had never been a fixed amount in the divorce settlement). Now I had no idea what the future would bring but I did have my tax refund cheques. I decided to give the state refund to Jackie while keeping the federal one to help get me through my initial transition. The wisdom of this decision was questioned when Jackie bought, among other things, a handmade quilt for $750 and took herself off to visit her Greek boyfriend in Rhodes while at the same time paying the airfare for Nick to come to stay with me in Ilford. She had obviously missed the point regarding child support.

My farewell to my parents was unemotional. I took a taxi to the airport and caught my flight, using my typewriter as hand luggage. I was glad to be leaving the Baltimore summer. On the day I left in July, the temperature was 95°F and the humidity a stifling 97%.

For some reason, I arrived feeling more jet lagged than on previous flights. At passport control I made the mistake of telling the truth when asked how long I planned to stay. I was stiffly informed that I should have sorted something out before travelling. I replied that I had indeed contacted the British Embassy in Washington and was given quite different information. The officer shrugged and advised me that as soon as I was married I should go to the Home Office and have my status updated.

I then retrieved my two suitcases and, somewhat laden down, stood in the crowded arrivals area and searched the throng for my beloved. I was a bit puzzled to see an attractive young Asian woman waving at me. I quickly realised that this was Diane, deeply tanned from her holiday which was accentuated by the very white Indian-style dress she was wearing. Her father, also with a mahogany tan, was with her and actually smiling. The emotional reunion was cut short by the reminder that we needed to get to Hampshire. The three of us managed to get through the crowd and to the car park. Then we were ready for the seventy-five mile journey to Fordingbridge.

Once in the car, I sat up front with Ron which gave me a front row seat to witness his driving skills. He was a very experienced and capable driver. He was also a big fan of Formula One racing and this obviously had an influence on him as he sped along, weaving in and out of traffic on highways that in America would have been considered side roads. It was literally an eye-opening experience and, at least momentarily, scared the jet lag out of me. As we neared our destination, I was amazed to find that old thatched cottages existed in real life and not just on travel posters. Peasash Farm, it turned out was not one of them.

The family residence sat in a large open space reached by the narrowest of country lanes. There were actually two houses, one older than the other, that were joined by a conservatory that also served as the entrance. Despite the name, it was not a working farm except for a modest veggie patch out the back. As soon as I got out of the car, I was greeted by Diane's mother with her usual exuberance. Once inside, there was just time to drop my luggage and have a quick bite of lunch before the four of us were back in the car for the drive to Ringwood, a distance of about six or seven miles.

The registry office was an unassuming little building with just a hint of officialdom. The only thing I remember about getting the special licence was a woman with a very posh voice saying: "Oh, you're the foreign divorce" on my arrival.

Peasash Farm – Annie and Ron lived in the house on the left,
Lynne and her family on the right with the conservatory in between.

Once we were back "home", I collapsed on the bed in the guest room where I was soon joined by Diane. The rest of the day remains a blissful blur in my memory.

We only stayed in Fordingbridge for a couple of days – just long enough to taste the very different atmosphere of an old English village and the countryside. Then Diane and I were driven to Southampton Station to catch a train to London. We had a lot to do and less than three weeks to do it in. We somehow managed to get all my stuff back to London and then to the flat. I was disappointed that Mum the cat did not seem to remember me. We were met by Diane's neighbour Martin who now had a live-in girlfriend, a bright and bouncy young thing named Carol. They also had a cat, another grey tabby known as Benjamin Bijou.

It was very good to be back in the flat and I felt very comfortable there. Diane, as always, had more energy than I did and was already happily chattering away about all the things we needed to do before we got married. But, for the moment, I was happy simply to be back where I felt I belonged.

====================================

SEVEN – A NEW LIFE

I could never understand why getting married needed to be so complicated. All right, so it is supposedly that happiest day in a woman's life but, come on, this was the third time for Diane. At least it was not going to be a big church wedding. The ceremony in the registry office was a much simpler one but, apparently, still required a fair amount of preparation and would also include a big celebration afterwards. I partly coped with it all by trying to remember all the jokes about being married I had ever heard. My favourite was: marriage is not a word, it's a sentence.

Among the essentials was, of course, the rings but this was relatively easy to sort out after an extended expedition to the jewellery shops in Oxford Street. Diane was happy with simple gold bands. What sort of wedding rings she had previously was a mystery as they had disappeared long before we met. The more involved decisions revolved around what to wear. I had brought a nice summer suit with me and needed only a new dress shirt, a tie, and some suitable shoes. Although I found what I wanted fairly easily, what I had not taken into consideration was the difference between American and British sizes in clothing. As a result, what I finally wore on the big day was a tad tighter than I was used to.

Finding a dress that pleased Diane, on the other hand, was a major operation. When I asked her what exactly she was looking for, she replied with typical Diane logic: "I'll know it when I see it." I think the search for the source of the Nile was probably easier than the search for Diane's wedding dress. We looked everywhere in Ilford, the West End and even down the market in Petticoat Lane. I cannot remember where we eventually found The Dress – a frilly, off the shoulder baby blue frock – but the important thing was that Diane loved it. Then she announced that she would also need a new dress for the party afterwards.

In case anyone was wondering, Diane and I still found time in the midst of all this to simply enjoy being together.

The curious thing is that Diane had often insisted that she never wanted to get married again and was only marrying me so that I could legally stay in the country. We often used to joke that eventually we could get divorced and just live together. Luckily, for all sorts of reasons, we stayed married. But first we had to get through the process.

As it turned out, Diane's parents would be celebrating their fortieth wedding anniversary two days after our wedding with Ron's birthday falling on the day in between. This was deemed sufficient cause for a big family celebration. So while our wedding would be a fairly small affair followed by a wedding breakfast back at Peasash, the really big party would take place that evening in the upstairs room at the venerable old George Inn in Fordingbridge, supposedly once a hangout for local highwaymen and smugglers. I would be meeting all of Diane's relatives at once which was a daunting prospect.

One thing we nearly forgot about was deciding on who was to be our witnesses – the best man and maid of honour. I hardly knew anyone so I asked our neighbour Martin to be my best man, assuring him it was a largely ceremonial role. Diane chose her friend and workmate Lorraine as her witness and it was Lorraine who would drive us to Hampshire the day before while Martin and Carol would come in their own car, presumably for a speedy getaway.

Lorraine's boyfriend Ron was not coming but he had given her a set of directions that was supposedly the easy route through London. Of course, she got hopelessly lost in the middle of town and we were well behind schedule by the time we got to the main road heading westward. We all silently hoped it was not an omen. When we got to Peasash there were already some family members there and I got out of the car and into a spotlight that would remain on me for most of the next two days.

The morning of the wedding was warm and sunny. Lynne's husband Brian was, among other things, a dealer in upmarket cars and he would be leading the procession to Ringwood in a white Rolls Royce. As the cars began to pull out, Diane was still inside putting on her finishing touches. The most amusing sight of the day was Diane running down the driveway and calling out "Wait for me!" as though anyone would leave without her.

The Wedding – signing the registry

I wish I had a better memory of the ceremony but I do recall that it was mercifully brief. In fact, we probably spent more time taking pictures outside afterwards. I do not think I ever saw Diane looking happier. In a moment of vanity, she had chosen not to wear her glasses so she clung to me not just as her new spouse but also a kind of guide dog. It was one of those occasions when the realisation of what was happening took a little while to sink in – the once tentative pen friends were now husband and wife. The wedding was not a happy ending but a bright and hopeful new beginning.

Diane told me years later that some people warned her that the marriage would never last. I like to think we stayed together because she loved me and not just to prove them wrong.

The happy couple and the white Rolls

Back at Peasash, the traditional English wedding breakfast in the conservatory was a fairly raucous affair in contrast to the usual American stereotype of the British being cool and reserved. At one point, they even tried to sing The Star Spangled Banner. The meal and the cake had been prepared by a local game keeper's wife who was slaving away unseen in Lynne's kitchen. Martin read out a few telegrams from well-wishers and I was asked to make a speech I was not prepared for and which I delivered with some surprising emotion.

Back at Peasash with Mum and Dad

After these festivities, Diane and I took ourselves upstairs. Annie had insisted that we have the big master bedroom for the occasion but we would have been just as happy in the guest room. We could hear that everyone was still having a good time downstairs but we were having quite a celebration of our own. We eventually had the best nap we ever had.

In the evening we got into our party gear and went with Annie and Ron to the George Inn, my first visit to a real English pub. The room upstairs was crowded with friends and family, had an open bar with snacks, and some slightly dated dance music blaring out of badly placed speakers. But it was a party. Since the occasion was just as much Annie and Ron's, we were glad not to be the only centre of attention. I was constantly being introduced to people who invariably asked "How do you like England?" to which my now standard reply was "I like any country that has Diane in it." I seemed to get along best with Diane's three younger female cousins which seemed to amuse her. I was sometimes left to mingle on my own while Diane danced, not necessarily with anyone, along to terrible songs like "Agadoo", the "Birdie Song" and "Superman" – all of which were (thankfully) new to me.

We had to drive back to Ilford the next day because Diane and Lorraine had to be back at work on Monday. Diane's father provided us with a more reliable set of directions and the journey was not only easier and quicker but more scenic. Martin and Carol had not stayed for the party so they had come home the night before, much to the relief of the two cats. It somehow seemed different now to be in the flat – that now I belonged although I always considered it to be Diane's flat. She was exhausted and only wanted to sleep. Her parents and I were very grateful that she had kept her sugar levels under control throughout the weekend.

While Diane had her nap, I remember standing at the window and looking out at that little corner of England and thinking: "Well, you've really done it now."

The next week would be busy. On one day, Diane had an appointment at Moorfields Eye Hospital. In the months before our marriage, she had been there for some laser treatment (she called it "zap guns") to repair some bleeding behind her eyes which was apparently a side effect of diabetes. This was something she had neglected to mention previously. She now needed to go back twice a year for check-ups to make sure the condition did not return. This involved photographing her eyes – a nasty procedure which has since been improved. To open the pupils of her eyes, she was given drops which blurred her vision for hours meaning she could not work that day and needed someone like me to accompany her home. My familiarity with the National Health Service was increasing all the time.

A couple of days later I made the journey to the immigration department of the Home Office at Lunar House in Croydon to apply for residency and permission to seek employment. It was a long drawn out process but I was given a one year probationary stamp in my passport and advised that I would also need to register my address and any employment with the police's Alien Registration Office in London.

We had a happier destination on Saturday, exactly one week after we were married, when we went to Covent Garden to see the Royal Ballet production of *Romeo and Juliet*. It was a wonderful performance of this most romantic of ballets and in the end the tears were freely flowing down Diane's cheeks.

Then, just one week after that, my son Nick arrived for a two week visit. His mother thought it would be good for the boy to see his father again while she was off in Rhodes enjoying herself. She seemed to have no qualms about a thirteen year old making a transatlantic flight – his first flight – on his own. She also did not consult me about his visit so much as inform me. Diane was initially uneasy, worried about how Nick would feel about her and also concerned about having three people in that little flat. She did not want to be viewed as some sort of wicked stepmother but ended up making jokes about precisely that.

I went to meet Nick at Gatwick who arrived early in the morning. He was tired but excited to be there and found riding on the trains something of a novelty. When we got to the flat and I introduced him to Diane there was none of the tension or unease I had expected. Diane was the nervous one but she quickly got over that by fussing over Nick, giving a brief tour, and making a light lunch. I use the word "light" because Diane was about to discover how much of an appetite growing American teenagers had.

One unexpected result of Nick's visit was that it gave me the chance to see at least a hint of the sort of mother Diane would have been. Even as a girl she had enjoyed frequently looking after her three younger cousins and, given the chance, she would have happily spoiled Lynne's children. I know she would have dearly loved to have had at least one child of her own and that child would never have been in doubt that it was loved. But during her time with Gerry she had a couple of miscarriages and these left her unable to conceive again. She and I did try to become parents – we tried very hard and with admirable enthusiasm and, in fact, never once used birth control – but it was not to be. I think not having children was probably Diane's biggest and possibly only regret. She once said to me, in a rare downcast moment: "What am I going to leave behind when I'm gone?" The only reply I had to such a question was simply to hold her.

The three of us went to Valentine Park the next day and Nick had a wonderful time feeding the squirrels. But during the week Diane would be at work so it would just be a father trying to entertain his son – a son who was appalled by British television having only four channels. I decided to take Nick to see some of the famous sights in London but I found that his interests did not necessarily coincide with mine. This became evident when we came out of the Underground station at Westminster. There in front of us were the Houses of Parliament and Big Ben but all that Nick seemed to notice was a poster for the film *Ghostbusters* on a nearby bus shelter. He showed a bit more interest at the Tower of London and actually seemed to enjoy doing a brass rubbing in Westminster Abbey but he also required frequent intakes of food and drink.

Diane suggested that we all go down to Fordingbridge that weekend which included the August bank holiday where Nick could socialise with some English kids. He got along well with all of Lynne's children. Danny, the oldest was only slightly younger than Nick and very outgoing. He even managed to get Nick to try playing cricket. Nick even got on with the two girls: Charlotte, who was about a year younger than Danny, and Hannah, a few years younger still who Nick seemed to delight in teasing. I only hoped my son was not being a bad influence but Annie thought the mini clash of cultures could only be a good thing. After all, it worked for Diane and me.

Back in London, Diane returned to work and I took Nick to the British Museum two days in a row because it was the first place he seemed to genuinely enjoy, especially the extensive Egyptian exhibits. As he got older, he became very interested in ancient Egypt and I like to think that fascination began on that trip.

I should mention that Jackie had given Nick some spending money for the trip and that he took every penny of it back to Baltimore with him. Nick was very proud of his talent for mooching.

Nick and the wicked stepmother

When it was time for Nick to leave, both Diane and I took him to the airport. Diane was worried about him flying on his own but Nick seemed more than okay with it. He was actually flying to New York where he would meet his mother so they could make the connecting flight to Baltimore together. Nick was lucky in that he easily found Jackie when they were both still in the baggage reclaim area. It had been mostly nice to have Nick visit but as we took the train back to London both Diane and I felt a sense of relief.

Mum the cat probably missed Nick more than we did. The two of them always seemed to be together in the flat and I think Mum even slept with Nick on the sofa-bed. She was the most affectionate feline I ever met – she wanted to love everybody. She had a rough time while I was in Baltimore. Diane took her to a vet who found she had a gum disease. The only cure was to remove all her teeth so Mum became a toothless moggy who could only eat very soft food. This did not stop her craving other delicacies. One time she was beside me on the sofa when I was eating a piece of Kentucky Fried Chicken. She fixed the stare of a huntress on me and suddenly a paw lashed out and snatched the chicken right out of my hands. She was probably only able the mumble down the skin but I learned to be careful about what I ate around her.

Meanwhile Diane had improved the control of her blood sugar levels with a new – to her – testing system. This was a tube of sticks on which she put a drop of blood from a pricked finger. The blood made two bands on the stick produce shades of green and tan, the darker the colours, the higher the sugar. On the side of the tube were samples of the different possible results. The idea was to match the colours on the stick to one of the ones on the tube which would indicate the blood sugar level. There was seldom an exact match and we frequently had a long discussion about what the actual result was but it was better than nothing. At least it gave us an early warning so that we could prevent the onset of a hypo.

I now got busy trying to find a job. The process was quite different to that in the states. In Baltimore, a job search usually began by scanning page after page of help wanted classified ads in the city's only newspaper. In London, there were many different newspapers with very limited ads. Instead there was a heavy reliance on employment agencies that were not all that encouraging. I had arrived at a time of high unemployment and some social unrest with things like a miners' strike going on. Out of work Americans were not exactly in demand but I felt sure that somebody somewhere would be looking for a person with my experience.

Diane was wonderfully encouraging and supportive and full of helpful suggestions. But I was worried that she might feel that she had fallen into the same situation as her previous marriage in which she seemed to take all the responsibility and provide most of the income. She continued to work overtime on two nights a week and on one occasion she and Lorraine spent most of a weekend in the office working on the documents for a very sensitive and high profile litigation case their bosses were handling. My supply of cash was running low but Diane never let me feel like I was a burden. I had not expected it would be easy to find a job in another country but Diane was always optimistic. She was fond of saying that the first two years of a marriage were the hardest. But we were still in the first two months.

After filling out applications and going to a few interviews, mostly in retail, I was offered a position with a company called Video Victoria run by a pirate named Dermot Ryan. At that time, home video was still quite new and films on tape were expensive so there was a sudden surge in video rental shops. Ryan had a large stock of videos in his location near Charing Cross which he rented, not to individuals, but to these shops. He also planned to open a shop of his own on Tottenham Court Road and was supposedly looking for a manager for it. In the meantime, I would help to organise and control the main stock.

From the start, I never felt comfortable in this place. I had encountered many shady characters in the music business but this Ryan was far shadier. Most of his staff was much younger than me and nearly all were under the impression they were to be the manager of the new shop. To my mind, the stock at Charing Cross did not seem sufficient to support the business. I was far from happy with the situation and left after three weeks. The only good thing about the experience was that I had earned enough money to keep going for a while and to contribute to our marital expenses. I thought Diane might be upset but she had enough bad jobs in her time to be understanding.

The relationship with Diane was a constant learning experience for both of us. The more we understood about one another, the closer we felt. I had never known someone who was as open and honest as Diane. She was not a saint and she was not perfect but she was everything I needed and I could only hope she felt the same way about me.

One thing I soon discovered was that Diane hated the month of October. At first I assumed that my little sun lover dreaded the changing of the seasons and the increasingly shorter days when the clocks changed from summer time. This was only part of it. October held memories for Diane of some of her darkest days from the bad old days. In particular, October 26th was the anniversary of her desperate suicide attempt. Because she survived it, she always referred to that day as her second birthday. I adopted the habit of always giving her a birthday card on that day – sometimes a pretty one, sometimes a funny one – on which I inserted the word "second" in between the "happy" and "birthday" (the word "love" also invariably appeared). It was a little gesture that she always appreciated.

When the calendar turned to December, the prospect of my securing a job suddenly improved. I got on the short list for the position of warehouse manager at the big Argos store on Oxford Street. At the same time, I came across a little ad in the *Evening Standard* for a records supervisor at a large firm of solicitors in the City. This really intrigued me. I had never worked in an office environment and I was not sure about returning to the world of retail. Diane told me about the records system in her firm and felt I was more than capable of handling a job like this. Not only that, we would be close to one another in the City and able to commute back and forth together. So I thought what the hell, applied for it, had a pleasant interview, and made it onto another short list. Everything seemed to be happening at once.

We were scheduled to spend the Christmas holiday with Diane's family in Hampshire and as we got deeper into the month there was no definite word from either job. Then, a few days before we were supposed to leave, I was offered the Argos job. It was success at last but by this time I found myself hoping the one at Linklaters & Paines would also come through. So I delayed accepting the Argos position, despite a couple of impatient phone calls from them, in the hope I would be equally successful with the other possibility.

It was only a day or two before we left that my future boss – a natty little Scottish chap named Alex Cook – phoned to say that I had the Linklater job and could I please report for work on January 2nd. I accepted with controlled excitement then rang the nice guy at Argos to politely decline their offer. So Diane and I could happily celebrate the holidays knowing that in the new year I would be, as they say, gainfully employed. A great weight had been lifted off me and I now felt relaxed enough to throw myself into the chaos of my first English Christmas.

And chaos it seemed to be. I borrowed a line from a film and remarked that I had seen better organised riots. But it was all in fun and the celebrations were largely based in the conservatory at Peasash where a long dining table had once again been set up beside a large and haphazardly decorated tree. In the morning – no, we did not go to church – a stream of local visitors came to see Lynne and Brian and were treated to drinks in their house while Diane and her mother were busily preparing the turkey and the rest of the meal in Annie's not very big kitchen. Ron, who had survived many of these occasions, wisely stayed out of the way. I thought I should be a good boy and offered to help in the kitchen but probably only got in the way.

The most vivid memory I had of that Christmas was when the preparations for the meal had reached a critical stage and Diane and Annie were becoming increasingly frantic. Into this potentially explosive scene wandered Lynne, slightly sloshed and holding a glass of champagne, who casually asked: "So what's happening with this dinner then?" How she escaped alive remains a mystery.

On the train back to London, Diane snuggled up to me and easily fell asleep while I reflected on the slightly eccentric events of the past few days and wondered what the future – and working in the City of London – would be like.

===================================

EIGHT – SETTLING IN

I could never have adapted to my unexpected change in career of working in a large British law firm without the help and advice of my wonderful Diane who sometimes found aspects of my transition to be mildly amusing. I soon found out that mine was a new position that was created to bring some order and discipline into the firm's records department. The staff was all young lads in their early twenties – four of them were permanent, six were long term temporaries, and there was a woman in her fifties who answered the phone and did light secretarial work. The duties of the department were carried out in a very carefree manner with time keeping a particular problem. My first task was to provide proper supervision. The fact that I immediately began to lay down rules and was an American besides did not endear me to this lot.

This is not the place to go into the details of my work history. It is enough to say that I was at Linklaters for thirteen years and experienced many ups and downs and had a swift education in office politics. I also had an insight into the British class system which was apparent all the way from the mail room to the partners' offices. In this regard, my being an American was an advantage in that I could not be regarded as one class or another and was able to interact with nearly everybody on a more or less equal basis.

I eventually was made redundant when cost conscious senior management decided to relocate my department to Colchester. This was followed by over two years at KPMG and then a five year stretch at another law firm, Ashurst Morris Crisp, where I had yet another newly-created position as an administrator. And all this time Diane was in the midst of her twenty-five years at Norton Rose.

Work is a boring subject which I will try my best to avoid in these pages except to say that the lower salaries – compared to my American jobs – was compensated for the surprising amount of paid holiday time which started at four weeks in the first year and gradually added days. And having two permanent incomes did nothing to harm the relationship with my lovely new wife and even allowed Diane to finally give up her regular nights of overtime. Of course, our work situations would change over the years but at this early stage everything was looking good.

Diane was happy that we could travel to and from work together. Her office was just a couple of blocks from Liverpool Street Station while mine was about a ten or fifteen minute walk farther into the City. We were close enough that we could sometimes have lunch together – if I could pry Diane away from her succession of very demanding bosses ("They always give me the difficult ones" she used to say). In the evenings we met at the station for the journey home. I was usually there first as Diane was prone to having last minute emergencies.

I became very familiar with the Barbican Centre which was a short distance from my office. In addition to its being the London base for the Royal Shakespeare Company, it also had a large concert hall, a cinema, gift shops, a couple of restaurants and a library. It occurred to me that it could be very convenient to go there after work and for a meal somewhere. Shortly after I started work I persuaded Diane to go to a concert by the Royal Philharmonic of some fairly light pieces with Ravel's *Bolero* as the climax. I knew that she liked that and she was enthralled to see and hear it performed live.

While symphonic concerts were not necessarily to Diane's taste – we also went to rock concerts elsewhere – she did like going to the Barbican both to see the RSC and to the rather plush cinema in the complex. We also found one of the restaurants to be quite reasonable for a pre-show meal. It was a handy place for a night out during the week and it was close enough to the station that we did not get home too late. A very good time was had and we were able to spend some quality time together in nice surroundings.

The Barbican Centre

We spent the long Easter weekend in Hampshire where Annie and Ron were in a wandering mood. They took us to nearby Breamore House, an Elizabethan manor with an even older Saxon church on the grounds, to the famous stately home of Broadlands (site of Chuck and Di's honeymoon), and I got to see Salisbury and its magnificent cathedral for the first time. As Diane's parents and I got to know each other better, I began to relax with them and genuinely enjoy their company. This was a great relief to Diane because she claimed we were her three most favourite people in the world (similarly, Annie once said that I was her favourite of all of Diane's husbands). Weekends in Hampshire would soon become a habit and a welcome respite from life and work in town.

In between we still had visits to Moorfields Eye Hospital and to the "ghoul clinic" in Whitechapel as well as occasional appointments with Diane's GP, a tiny Indian woman with a ridiculously long name and a ridiculously small surgery just outside the side entrance to Ilford Station. When I think of all the insulin, syringes and other stuff that Diane got free prescriptions for I could not fail to wonder what it would have cost if we lived in the good old USA.

Have I mentioned how much I loved Diane? She used to say to me: "Tell me that you love me – as if you really mean it" and I would dutifully reply: "I love you – as if I really mean it". Such banter usually led on to other things. At the risk of sounding slightly crude, our sex was so good that the neighbours had a cigarette afterwards.

As we celebrated our first anniversary, it was pointed out that we had never had a honeymoon or a holiday together. Annie and Ron decided to rectify that by inviting us on a three week holiday to the south of France in their motor caravan. Despite some hesitation about three weeks with my in-laws and living in a caravan I agreed because, if nothing else, a trip to France was bound to be worth it, especially with my Diane.

I have written previously about the holiday adventures Diane and I had over the years and I hesitate to repeat myself too much here. In addition to the wonderful and occasionally raucous time we had, I really became part of Diane's family on that trip. She had always told me that Annie and Ron were more like friends than parents and I certainly found that out for myself during those three weeks. I began to feel closer to them than to my actual parents and the feeling seemed to be reciprocated. Ron told me that he and Annie were both happy and relieved that Diane had finally found someone who would take care of her.

Diane was equally happy to have dragged me into the sun. I was never one for lying on beaches but Diane was having none of that. She was a sun lover from way back and she was determined that I was going to strip off and be in the sun with her. In one of her early letters, Diane had written about her love affair with the sun, especially the warm Mediterranean sun, and then added: "I do love a man with a tan". That line initially worried me with my permanently pale body but then I thought: what the hell, we're never going to meet anyway. Getting me to have a tan was just one of the many ways that Diane changed my life. I would do anything to make her happy – well, almost anything.

That first holiday

Although Diane and I had many likes and dislikes in common, we also had plenty of differences which were only natural considering our different backgrounds. I had been obsessed with movies ever since I was a little kid and during the Sixties I went to see every British film that was showing. Diane, meanwhile, turned out to be a big fan of Clint Eastwood whose films I had mostly ignored. She also loved horror flicks, especially those with vampires. So we spent a lot of time exposing each other to our favourites. I was glad that she loved Laurel and Hardy and the Antoine Doinel films of François Truffaut. She was less impressed with musicals although she did enjoy – when she was in the right mood – Gene Kelly movies (she hated Fred Astaire and called him "monkey man"), *West Side Story,* and she never tired of seeing one of my all-time favourites, *Li'l Abner.* While on the subject of movies, I should mention that Diane was never able to watch *E.T.* without shedding a bunch of tears.

One film I shared with Diane was *The Americanization of Emily,* a wartime comedy/drama about an American guy and an English girl starring James Garner and Julie Andrews, a movie I had loved since I first saw it in the Sixties. This was Julie Andrews before she began sugary sweet. I knew her from the cast albums of *Camelot* and *My Fair Lady* and had seen her performing songs from both shows on the old Ed Sullivan show when I was about twelve or thirteen. I was quite taken with her and thought how nice it would be to have my own Julie Andrews, a feeling strengthened by seeing her in the film. As time went by, this feeling faded as I found other distractions and interests. But just recently I began to think that, in an odd sort of way, I had found my Julie Andrews in Diane. My darling wife, of course, would have hated the comparison no matter how tenuous but I think it was just one of the many reasons why I loved her. I would never have wanted to Americanize her but I think we were a prime example of the USA/UK's special relationship.

Music was another area where our tastes both coincided and widely varied. I had been brought up listening to recordings of Broadway shows and classical music. In my teens, I was more interested in jazz than rock although I eventually saw the error of my ways. Diane, of course, loved rock and heavy metal and listened to everything from Bob Dylan to the Eagles to Pink Floyd and, somewhat surprisingly, Roxy Music. Unlike me, she preferred the Rolling Stones to the Beatles (she hated Paul McCartney for which I could not blame her). She knew all the lyrics from Ian Hunter's solo albums. Diane was in heaven when we had front row balcony seats to see Hunter and Mick Ronson at the Dominion Theatre. She was always jealous of all the concerts I got to see for free during my days in the record business. For the most part, I shared these tastes but not so much Led Zeppelin, Hawkwind and the like. But we both agreed as time went on that very little decent music had emerged since the end of the Seventies.

In addition to working and being madly in love with Diane, I managed to find some time to continue my attempts at creative writing. I joined a play writing workshop at City University in Islington and became intrigued by the notion of writing plays for radio. To make a long story shorter (it is something else I have written about elsewhere) I was inspired to write a short two character radio play called *The Long Goodnight Kiss* about a couple trying to settle down for the night but never managing to get to sleep. I sent the script to the BBC and, after a long wait, it was accepted which led to an even longer wait before it was recorded and broadcast. But after only a couple of years in England, the BBC was producing something I had written. Diane was very proud of me which was the best reward – although the nice payment did not hurt either.

After I had been working for a year, the Home Office changed my status to that of a permanent resident of the UK. It was also about this time that Diane and I realised that, as charming as her flat was, it really was not big enough for the both of us. We began looking at the listings in estate agents' windows – seeming to decide without much discussion to stay in or near Ilford – with an eye on much larger flats. Then we agreed that the really sensible thing to do would be to get a house.

We had the expected mixed results while house hunting. Some were mildly interesting while others were simply dumps. One was inhabited by some Asian guys who had mattresses on the floor instead of furniture while another still had a working outside toilet. Estate agents in Britain are far less helpful than those in America. They mostly just advertise what is for sale or rent and tell you when you can go and have a look at them. At that time, the property market was booming and For Sale signs seemed to be everywhere. We explored bits of Ilford I had never seen and eventually went to see a house on Perth Road, which bordered Valentine Park but was still a short distance from it.

The house was part of the so-called Commonwealth Estate, an area fancied by people who worked in London and featured street names of cities such as Brisbane, Quebec, Auckland, Melbourne and so on. The houses with their spacious gardens were built in the Edwardian era when the train line to London made commuting possible. The house we looked at was lived in by an older Jewish couple who were planning to spend their retirement in Spain. Unlike many houses along the road, it still had a front garden instead of paved parking spaces.

Number 20 Perth Road, Ilford

Diane instantly loved the house. She said she was very sensitive to the aura of places and liked the feeling within this one. Her mother said she had done much the same thing when they first viewed her flat. As soon as they walked in the door, Diane had said "I'll have this" before seeing all of it. The same thing seemed to happen here but she was thankfully much quieter about it. If she had any doubts, they disappeared when she saw the ninety foot long back garden. We rushed back to the estate agent and immediately put a deposit on the house. That, needless to say, was the easy part.

The first things we had to do was to arrange a mortgage and then to sell Diane's flat. Since we both had good, steady jobs it was not too difficult to obtain a mortgage. The one we got was called an endowment mortgage which was very popular at the time but had the nasty habit of biting you in the ass twenty-five years later. When an estate agent came to assess the flat, we were surprised – no, shocked – to learn that the property market was such that the value of the flat had more than doubled in the four years since Diane bought it. The sale would provide the down payment for the house and then some. All we needed was a buyer.

The eventual buyer was an unsmiling, middle-aged woman who said she wanted something in the area so that she could be near her apparently wayward daughter. She was quite sniffy as she looked around the flat but I thought she was merely trying to conceal her interest. Diane did most of the talking because it was, after all, her flat. I was surprised that Diane was so nervous in this situation and amazed that her negotiating skills seemed to consist of immediately say "yes" to all demands. Thus we were committed to painting all the walls in a very neutral magnolia colour. For some reason, for years afterwards Diane always laughed at the mention of the word "magnolia".

As much as Diane loved the new house (new to us – it was built in 1905) she was still sad at leaving her little flat which not only held some nice memories but which had also been a symbol of her hard fought independence.

On the evening before our move, I went to the house to collect the keys from the previous owners, the Hirsts. One half of the couple – Mrs. Hirst – seemed less enthusiastic about going than the other. My visit coincided with some activity in the back garden where it was not yet dark. Hirst took me out and introduced me to my new neighbour, a large black South African with a booming voice he called Ted. It turned out that Ted was an obsessive gardener who had persuaded the Hirsts, who had no interest in gardening, to let him have the run of their back garden which was much larger than his. This explained Diane's impression that while the house keeping seemed to leave something to be desired, the garden looked immaculate. This Ted was in the process of closing the gap he had made in the fence to allow his access. I should have guessed from his overall manner that Ted would turn into a major nemesis.

The move went easily enough although it confused the hell out of Mum the cat. We had bought some new furniture and more would be delivered in the coming days as well as a large freezer. We also bought a large pine dresser and matching dining table from the Hirsts and we needed to replace the kitchen window sooner rather than later. The house was somewhat eccentric. It had obviously undergone various transformations, some more successful than others, and nothing ever seemed to be a standard size. Diane liked the fact that the house still had a separate sitting room and dining room. There had been a fad in the Seventies to demolish the connecting wall between these two to create a "through lounge" that extended from the front of the house to the back. Diane much preferred the cosiness of a contained sitting room and I tended to agree with her.

There were only two bedrooms upstairs – the large master bedroom and a smaller one that would become my den. What was probably once a third bedroom had been divided into a bathroom and a utility room containing a washing machine and dryer, appliances many homes had in the kitchen. Diane, who was well known for the occasional malaprop, once referred to the utility room as the "artillery room" and it was called that forevermore. Then there was the boiler which controlled the heating and hot water. This was an old dinosaur that was mounted on the wall in the master bedroom. Again, this was something that was not usually found upstairs in a British home. One thing I really missed was the lack of a basement but we had a loft. Many people converted their loft into extra rooms. We never did.

Whatever oddities the house contained, Diane loved the garden which would become her island of peace and sanity. At the end of it was a small rockery out of which grew a huge horse chestnut tree which turned bright red with flowery candles in the spring. About two thirds up the garden was a small pond that was actually an old bathtub no doubt installed by Ted. When we moved in there were actually a few goldfish swimming around in the pond's slightly murky waters. Mum the cat soon devoured the fish – probably swallowing them whole – and the tub eventually sprung a leak. It gradually filled with weeds and a few wildflowers and despite its lack of water was still referred to as the pond.

One nice thing about the gardens along this stretch of road was that they did not face another row of houses and gardens. Instead the gardens were bordered by a high brick wall that had once been part of an electricity substation. Thus there was more privacy than usual. We were similarly fortunate in the front where instead of facing other houses we were across the street from a C. of E. church. And while we had Ted as a neighbour on one side, the house on the other side was empty. It had apparently belonged to an old man who died and his son chose to do nothing with it except to occasionally use it for storage. Its back garden was a wild and overgrown jungle full of weeds, brambles and berry bushes that provided a kind of barrier but also required constant cutting back from our side. So, like everywhere else in the known universe, the house had its advantages and disadvantages. One of the latter was that it was a much longer walk to Ilford Station and the shops.

The garden as it appeared a few years later

When we were still relatively young and reasonably fit, the daily fifteen to twenty minute walk to the station was not too much of a problem, except when the weather was against us. The walk home after working and commuting always seemed to take longer. But doing it together seemed to make it easier. We were able to chat and encounter various neighbourhood cats, one of which always wanted to follow us. One summer evening, it began to rain just as we began to make our way up the road. It was a passing shower and we were actually able to follow it all the way home without getting wet as it moved along in front of us. Diane remembered that episode as evidence that the gods were on our side.

In those days, we did a lot of walking at home and on holiday. It was Diane's favourite form of exercise. Occasionally, our ability to walk long distances came in handy. A snowstorm had hit London while we were at work. It was not the sort of storm I experienced during Baltimore winters but any amount of snow tends to bring London to a halt. As the offices emptied, it was obvious the transport network was unable to cope. There were no trains running. British Rail later explained that the reason was not because it was snowing but that it was "the wrong kind of snow".

The underground station was jammed but there was no guarantee its trains would do any better on the outlying stretches where the underground was actually above ground. Taxis were the first thing to disappear. Once Diane and I managed to meet in the midst of the chaos, we decided to try our luck elsewhere. So, along with a few other hardy souls, we trudged our way towards Whitechapel High Street in hopes of finding a taxi there. By the time we reached the hospital, we realised this was a fruitless quest.

We both agreed that it was better to keep moving than to stand still. That way we could at least create some warmth. We set off towards Mile End. The snow on the pavement was beaten down by numerous other pedestrians, many of whom resembled the living dead. I think we managed to get some coffee at a café along the way but we somehow – after how much time I have no idea – found ourselves on the outskirts of Stratford. The station was of no use except that it was also the site of a bus depot. We managed to get a bus going to Ilford and thawed out on the slow journey up Romford Road. The bus deposited us near Ilford Station and the rest of the trek was along a very familiar route. We were seldom so relieved to be in our warm house. The cat looked at us with a feline expression of "where the hell have you been?"

Diane was really in her element in organising everything. She was a virtual whirlwind of energy and activity and she seemed to enjoy every second of it. I was seeing a new and lovable side of my darling wife. She was not only happy, she was stronger.

While Diane and I had a very loving relationship, in those first few years of marriage there was a part of her that never seemed to fully trust her feelings or mine. This was very much the legacy of her time with Gerry which had left her with near-zero self-confidence and an inability to completely believe in others. It took me years to re-build Diane's self-confidence and I was never certain I was totally successful.

One of the worst and most lasting effects Gerry inflicted upon her was to give her a phobia about her weight. Diane always had a nice slim and supple body – one that I frequently praised in English, French and Braille – but she was forever worried about putting on weight and becoming what she considered to be fat. When she was with Gerry, she was even thinner than she was when we were married (everybody was thin in the Seventies) but Gerry used to ridicule her if she added so much as a pound. This paranoia never seemed to go away no matter how much I assured her that she was being silly about it. I even told her that she was too neurotic to ever get fat but it was one of those things – like trying to get her to give up smoking – that she seemed unable to change her mind about. I suspect that one of the causes of her various hypos was her not eating as much as she needed to because she was worried about gaining weight. This was just one of the many scars she had from the life before I knew her.

As much as I may have wanted to, I could not place all of the blame for Diane's troubles on Gerry. There was another person with whom Diane had a brief but disastrous relationship with soon after leaving Gerry. This evil individual took full advantage of Diane's vulnerability and made her feel worthless, even destroying some of her personal possessions in an attempt to control her. She almost never talked about this experience but it was bad enough for her to want a protection order against the nutcase. Her mother went with her when she met with the solicitor to explain the grounds for wanting the order. Annie was not in the room when Diane explained her ordeal but she told me that when the solicitor emerged from the meeting his face was ashen with shock.

When she moved into her flat, Diane was at least partly on the road to recovery. Now she had a new relationship and a new house. We were no longer living in a place that was hers but one that was ours. It really was a new beginning. I do not think either of us had a thought about how long we would live there.

NINE – HOME AND A VISIT TO BALTIMORE

We were becoming very domesticated. Diane and I suddenly acquired an interest in doing minor home improvements and Diane was positively giddy with delight when she discovered a B&Q do-it-yourself store within easy walking distance. It was a phase that would thankfully lose its novelty value but until then we busied ourselves with little projects when we could have been doing something more enjoyable. I mean, what are weekends for anyway?

The general décor of the house could be politely described as dated with a touch of shabby – not shabby chic, just shabby. It is perhaps to our shame but not necessarily to our regret that we did little to re-decorate. There was a good reason for this. We both worked very hard and when our holiday time came around we always preferred to go away to sunny and interesting places rather than staying home and doing even more work. That probably sounds lazy and selfish but it was how we survived the hassles of the rest of the year. The wisdom of this decision became apparent when we undertook to install all new kitchen cabinets, counters and a sink. Let us just say the project was a limited success but still an improvement on what we had before.

No one could ever accuse Diane of being a domestic goddess, especially in the days when we were both working. Housework was an occasional rather than a regular duty – and I admit I was not much help in that department. Diane had certain standards. They may have been low but she had them. For instance, she insisted on keeping the kitchen clean. But there were other things, such as sewing, which she either disliked or was not very good at. She had a sewing box with needles, threads and other bits but it was only opened as a last resort. We both enjoyed the memory of the time a button came off a shirt I was putting on and Diane just smiled and said: "Don't worry, babe, I'll buy you a new one."

When the weather was pleasant, Diane loved to be in the garden either lying on her lounger with a good book or puttering around the flowerbeds. If the den was my cave, the garden was definitely Diane's domain. I cut the grass and trimmed back anything she pointed at but the rest of the garden was hers to do with as she liked. She did not want her flowerbeds to look too formal or regimented but preferred a more natural look – what she used to call her wildlife garden. It certainly attracted birds and butterflies. In the front garden the main feature was a trio of rose bushes. But out back there was a variety of colour and some surprises such as bright red poppies that kept appearing in odd places.

Diane in the garden

The only thing Diane did not like was the comments and advice neighbour Ted was constantly calling over the fence to her (it was interesting that he would quickly disappear if I came out). Diane eventually pretended that she could not hear him and he went away. But his intrusion so annoyed her that one day when complaining to me about him she called him "Fuckface". We both laughed at that and it became his nickname from that point on although we usually abbreviated it to "F-F" if someone else was around.

I think that Fuckface used to kind of fancy Diane which is understandable to anyone who saw his wife who we dubbed "Butch". He would often come out when Diane was in the garden and more than once when he was doing something in the front and Diane walked by on some errand or other, he would stop what he was doing and watch her until she was out of sight. When I mentioned this to Diane she thought it was equal parts creepy and hilarious. It certainly did not stop her from occasionally sunbathing topless in the garden.

Now that we had the house, we made fewer trips to Hampshire but we were able to entertain guests, including Diane's parents who would come up for an overnight stay on weekends. Sometimes it was strictly for a visit but other times it was so the four of us could go to Earl's Court for something like the Caravan Show or the Ideal Home Exhibition. Diane enjoyed preparing the meals and occasionally also baked a cake. In the evenings the main entertainment was usually a video such as a taped performance by Billy Connolly who Annie and Ron thought was hilarious despite the language.

Diane had advised me not to show films with plots because she said her father had trouble following them and would be constantly asking "who's that" or "what's going on?" I am not sure how true that was although it was a running joke that Ron thought every American actor was Jack Palance. One time there was actually a movie on the box with Jack Palance and when Ron asked who it was I told him it was Kirk Douglas. If I really wanted to wind Ron up, all I had to do was casually mention how the Americans won the war.

I remember one warm pleasant afternoon when Diane's parents were visiting us. We were all in the dining room with the back door open. Diane started to make her usual fuss about preparing lunch and I sat at the keyboard and played old songs like *I Can't Give You Anything But Love, Baby.* I glanced up and saw Annie and Ron dancing on the patio and Diane standing in the doorway with a big smile on her gorgeous face. It was a really nice moment.

We had a proper sized sofa in the sitting room so the old sofa-bed was moved to the den. It was only marginally comfortable but good enough for a single night's stay. It was where my son Nick would sleep on subsequent visits. He came for another two week stay in the summer which was somewhat complicated by the fact that both Diane and I were working. Nick, being fifteen, insisted he was capable of taking care of himself. My old diary from that year has notations that on a couple of days Nick went to the British Museum and some of the other museums along "museum row" in Kensington but there is nothing to indicate how he got there or if we went with anybody. I know on one of his trips he spent some time with the kids of one of Diane's workmates who took him to Brighton one day and taught him the art of shoplifting. (Their mother was a loony leftie who once said to Diane: "I hope my daughter marries a nice black man someday" – but that's another story).

Anyway, Diane and I did take a couple of days off so we could take Nick on a long weekend to Hampshire. He always seemed very happy there and stayed for a couple of days on his own. Annie took him to the train at one end and I met him at the other. On his last Sunday in London, the three of us went to the zoo in Regents Park, the zoo being the traditional destination for divorced dads to take their kids. When it was time for him to leave, I took Nick to the airport. This time his flights were to and from the hell that is Heathrow which involved a seemingly endless journey on the Piccadilly Line.

We still had a few holidays with Diane's parents. There was an interesting and sometimes soggy trip to the Cotswolds in the big caravan and two trips down to Lynne's holiday apartment in Spain in which we travelled in Ron's new van. But after that our holidays were just the two of us except for one time Annie and Ron joined us for a trip to Menorca, despite their dislike of flying.

By that time, Diane quite enjoyed flying, in particular the take-off. But she did not fly for the first time until she was forty and that was the longest flight we ever made together. As I have already mentioned, I have written an entire book about our wonderful and occasionally weird holidays around Europe so I do not want to repeat myself here. That is a difficult decision to make because some of our very best times together were on these holidays. So if you really want to know about them, you will just have to get the other book (how's that for a shameless plug?). But there was one trip that was not included in the book because it was not to anywhere in Europe. It was my return and Diane's introduction to Baltimore in 1990.

I was never quite sure what my parents thought about that visit because they always tried to conceal their emotions. It was certainly something different for them as having people stay not just overnight but for two weeks was a new experience. Meanwhile, Diane was a bundle of nerves and excitement. She did not know how she would react to being on a plane although once we began to taxi and the engines started to thrust, she was ecstatic at finding a new thrill that did not involve drugs or sex. Her other main concern was how to handle her injections and all that since her body would have to adjust to a different time zone. The solution was to start five days ahead of time by moving up her injections an hour a day.

We sat at the very back of the plane which was the smoking section (remember them?). The big TWA jet was far from full and we felt almost on our own. A cheerful male attendant took little breaks in a seat across the aisle and chatted to us. He was very attentive and kept Diane well supplied with coffee. I worried that she would become restless on such a long flight but she coped well by regularly stretching her legs. Then when we were flying over Maine, the plane suddenly jumped and shook with a massive jolt. The attendant, who was in the aisle holding a pot of coffee, dropped to the floor and stayed there. The pilot informed everyone that we had hit turbulence which would hopefully soon clear. For the next few minutes, we felt like we were on a rollercoaster. I tried to assure Diane, whose eyes were wider than I had ever seen them, that this was not a usual part of flying.

It was a relief to land safely on a very sunny day. It was May and much warmer in Maryland than in England. We got through the formalities quickly and Diane remarked about how friendly everyone was. As we continued our journey in a taxi, Diane marvelled at the size of American highways, her first indication of just how different a country this was. We arrived at my parents' house in one piece and I made the unnecessary introduction of my wife to her in-laws. Diane likes to hug and kiss but she seemed to instinctively realise that might not be a good idea, at least not yet. We had some light refreshments and Diane gazed about at the environment from which I had come. By the time we finally went up to my old room to unpack, the long day was finally catching up with Diane and she whispered to me: "I'm hating every minute of this." I said nothing but thought to myself – this is going to be fun.

Diane's mood improved after a nap and then we went downstairs to discuss meals. My mother knew that Diane was diabetic but was unsure about what she could and could not eat. Even though I knew how much my mother hated anyone else using her kitchen, I suggested we could do our own meals. There was a practical reason for this. My parents had their meals early – dinner at 6pm for example – whereas Diane needed to wait to eat until after her injection at 7:30. So it would make sense to eat in shifts as it were although the four of us usually sat at the table for both meals. I also said that we would do our own food shopping because I wanted Diane to see an American supermarket for herself.

Within sight of the house was a small shopping centre with a Giant supermarket. Giant was the brand name but to Diane it was giant in both size and variety. Diane and her parents had always teased me about my sense of wonder when going to Europe but now I was able to do the same to Diane with a look on her face like Dorothy just arriving in Oz. Diane was especially amazed to discover an entire aisle of diet and non-sugar products. In the end, she admitted to being overwhelmed by choice.

Diane with my parents and Nick

I suppose the best word for the first couple of days would be tentative as my parents gradually got used to Diane's bubbly personality (and accent) and she learned that I had not exaggerated in descriptions of my parents and their nature. After the two dinners, we all sat in the living room and talked and Diane actually got some genuine laughs when telling stories about some of our European adventures. The four of us were learning to co-exist and there was a more relaxed atmosphere but still one without hugs. But I also wanted Diane to see some of Baltimore and to have a real American experience.

My father thought a good place to begin was a big shopping mall and offered to drive us to White Marsh which was one of the biggest at that time. Diane thought the parking lot around the mall was as big as Ilford and continued to be knocked out by what she found inside. My father dropped us off at one of the entrances and we arranged to meet again in a few hours. Diane was about to discover where the American Dream was bought and sold.

White Marsh was huge and on several levels. Once inside, there was no way of knowing the time of day or the season of the year. The mall had several large department stores and countless other stores of all sizes and descriptions. I remember when White Marsh first opened it boasted nineteen different shoe stores. It was late morning on a weekday but the place was bustling. I do not think we actually bought anything because Diane could not stop just looking. After a while, I suggested getting some lunch and we went upstairs to the food court which was the size of what the British laughingly called a mall.

Not only was Diane fascinated by the variety of food on offer but she was even more amazed by the quantities. She decided she only wanted a coffee and a salad. At each of these vendors, she asked for a small one, got quizzical looks and was repeatedly asked: "Are you sure you want a *small* one?" As we sat at a table, she commented that her "small" salad could probably feed a family. She then had a chance to look around at the spectacle of Americans devouring lunch.

While White Marsh was interesting, I wanted Diane to see some of the city including some places I had told her about. So our next foray was to take a bus to downtown – an experience in itself. To me, it was a very familiar route that went past my old high school, the library where I had my first job, and two of my old apartments. But what I really wanted to show her was Harborplace – a sparkling centrepiece of the new Baltimore that partially surrounded a bit of waterfront with open space, two large pavilions of shops and restaurants, a science museum, an aquarium, a big hotel and a couple of old ships such as a World War Two submarine and a man-of-war from the Revolution. Everything was clean and bright there but a few blocks in each direction was quite a different story.

Harborplace turned out to be Diane's favourite place in Baltimore and we returned them several times even having dinner in one of the restaurants once or twice. Diane particularly loved a coffee bar whose variety was staggering and where she enjoyed rich Colombian coffee (a small one, of course). We also toured the aquarium and saw an Imax film at the science centre but the sight Diane most remembered was of someone she saw as we strolled around. It was a "dude" – a very hip black guy in what looked like a red crushed velvet suit and matching cowboy hat, complete with sunglasses and walking stick and deep in conversation with a couple of strangely attired black girls who we assumed were business associates. Diane could not take her eyes off this person – she thought such people only existed in movies. "Quick, take a picture," she whispered but I decided not to take a chance. Diane did not really need a photo anyway – for years she would suddenly say to me: "Remember the dude?"

Diane and new friend in downtown Baltimore

One day we took a water taxi to a quite different part of town called Fells Point about which I had varied memories. It was once comprised of ethnic neighbourhoods – my mother grew up not far from there – but now had become rather trendy. Diane was tempted by a boutique called Cowboy Buddha – a name I would subsequently steal. She saw a kind of old gold coloured suit that she really liked. It was being examined by another woman but as soon as she put it back on the rack, Diane grabbed it and disappeared into the changing room. When she came out, she looked gorgeous. The other woman, who was still there, gave her a quick, jealous glance and murmured "That looks good on you." Diane bought the suit and wore it for years and was always asked where she had bought it. The shop also had some fantasy-type items so we added a small pewter wizard and a miniature crystal ball to our purchase. The crystal ball sat on a pewter stand that featured three skulls with red eyes. When Diane showed this to my mother, the response was: "Hmm, that's interesting." The wizard and the crystal ball are still in our sitting room.

Even though we were enjoying ourselves, we were not trying to avoid my parents and, in fact, spent quite a lot of time with them. I think they had finally decided that they liked Diane and she understood that their slightly cool, non-touching manner was nothing personal. We were occasionally joined by Nick who one time offered to take us to my old house in his very battered old car.

I could not believe that a house could change so much in six years and Diane could not believe that people could live in such a place. Jackie, never one for housework, had turned into a major hoarder. She had always wanted "things" and if someone was getting rid of something, she would have it. There was stuff everywhere – even the stairs had little piles of paper and bits on every step. The dining room was a monument to clutter with stacks of old newspapers in a corner. The large living room, one of the best features of the house, was so full of disorganised stuff, including another dining room table, that there was only a narrow pathway through it. Even worse was the kitchen with an overflowing rubbish bin and dirty dishes piled everywhere. We did not dare look in the fridge.

There was more of the same upstairs. Clothes were everywhere in the bedroom while a telephone was now mounted on the wall in the bathroom next to the toilet. The room that had once been my den was now covered from floor to ceiling with all sorts of stuff – all you could do was open the door. Nick had now made a home for himself in the basement and he suggested that we go there. On the way, he asked Diane if she would like a cup of coffee and she replied: "Only if I can wash the cup." We did not linger long but before leaving I took some pictures because I knew no one would believe us otherwise.

Jackie's living room

Our visit did not seem to stir much interest in other members of my family. The exception was Aunt Theresa and Uncle Joe who came over one evening. Theresa was my mother's sister - some people used to think they were twins – and Joe was a very typical little Italian with an eye for the ladies. I could never figure out how the two of them got together. It was a very pleasant evening with the six of us sat round the dining room table (I still had my assigned chair) having coffee and cake. Diane and Joe provided much of the mirth and they even seemed to twinkle at each other. When Diane went out on the front porch to have a cigarette – it was the only place where she could smoke – Joe followed her like a puppy. I could tell Joe was fascinated by her. For her part, Diane was flattered and amused to finally meet someone she could be herself with.

When it came time for us to go home there was more relief than sadness all around. We had called for a taxi to take us to the airport but as it got later and later there was no sign of it. My father finally said he would take us and we quickly piled our stuff into his car, but not before Diane finally gave me mother a hug and called her Sophie. My father had always been a nervous driver, the complete opposite to Diane's father, and he chose to go through town rather than take the beltway around. Still, he got us there on time and Diane almost laughed out loud when he said: "Sorry I had to drive like a maniac." We said goodbye and proceeded to do all the obligatory pre-flight stuff. Diane once again enjoyed the take-off and then slept most of the way. We talked a little bit about that trip from time to time over the years but I often wondered what Diane really thought about the experience. My main regret about that trip is that I never took Diane to Washington because I think she would have really enjoyed that.

I have not been back to Baltimore or the United States since.

===================================

TEN – CATS AND BOOKS

I want to say a few words about cats – they are crazy. Despite this fact, Diane and I loved cats. I never had one when I was growing up because my mother considered animals to be dirty. Diane's family seemed to have various pets over the years and her father was also a great cat lover. When I first went to the family home in Hampshire, I encountered Dazpuss (or Daz Puss) a great lump of fur that always seemed to be motionless on a certain chair quietly watching the world through narrow eyes. He was not a particularly sociable creature and I was advised that only Ron could touch him safely. Even so, when old Daz eventually passed away, Ron was upset for days and never had another cat although he enjoyed befriending others.

Some people wonder what is the good of cats. To the casual observer they do little more than eat and sleep – especially sleep. The worst thing that could happen to a cat is to develop insomnia. There was a cartoon in which one cat was saying to another: "Sorry about my bad mood. I only had sixteen hours sleep." But people who had a cat – a nice cat – felt differently. For one thing, most cats are terrific listeners. You can talk to a cat about anything and all they will do in return is stare at you and occasionally blink.

Our little Mum was the most affectionate cat I had ever known. When she was awake, she always seemed to be beside one of us. Her preferred place to sleep was in someone's lap. She used to stand on my chest and nuzzle my chin – Diane said she liked the feel of my beard. But I can remember more than one time when Diane was having an afternoon nap and Mum was curled up on the bed beside her. Mum had a gentle temperament despite having a rough earlier life. No wonder Diane liked her so much. Sadly, she was only with us for seven years. We buried her in the garden in the shade beneath the tree and I think we were both surprised at how emotional we felt.

But before Mum left us we had been adopted by another moggy, a rather serious looking black stray that wandered into our garden and decided he liked it there. Although he was feral, he was not mean. If we tried to pet him, he did not spit or lash out but simply kept lowering his head with a silent plea that seemed to say: "Please don't". Once we fed him for the first time, he became a regular visitor and we named him Dimly. In the morning Diane would find him outside the back door patiently waiting for his breakfast. He was such a character that we found it easy to indulge him. Mum was wary at first but the two cats soon decided they could co-exist, but at a distance.

Mum and Dimly

I was surprised by how much Diane liked Dimly – his nature really seemed to appeal to her. One warm day she had the back door open while she was doing something or other in the kitchen and there was a tape of Pink Floyd playing in the background. Dimly sat in the doorway and Diane insisted that he had his eyes closed and was grooving to the music. Since Dimly had no interest in coming inside, we bought a small wooden doghouse and this became his shelter and sleeping place in bad weather. But Dimly was not a permanent resident. He would sometimes disappear for days or even weeks at a time. One time he was gone for months and we thought we had seen the last of him. Then one morning there he was – sitting outside the door waiting for breakfast. As this was after Mum's passing, we were very glad to see him.

Dimly very seldom meowed. The only time he made any sort of noise was when walking away after eating. Diane was not sure if it was a meow or a fart. He had a funny kind of walk that suggested that he had been injured at some point in his life. In many ways, he was the ultimate stray and we missed him when he once again disappeared for a very long time. When he finally returned, he was not well. "He's come back to us to die" Diane sighed. I took half a day off to take him to a vet but when I got home Dimly was nowhere to be seen. I searched but never found him. He was his own cat right to the end.

We had barely recovered from Dimly when another weird cat appeared. We began to wonder if our garden was listed in some kind of guide book for cats. This one was a huge fluffy white thing that looked more like a small sheep than a cat. It did not seem to be a stray and was quite used to people. There were frequently notices about lost cats posted in the neighbourhood but I never saw one for this one. We speculated that it had been kicked out because it ate too much.

The big white thing

This cat was not bashful about coming down to the patio where it sniffed around, inspected the doghouse and indicated that it was all acceptable. Diane and I debated whether to feed it – it looked like it had eaten enough to last weeks – and whether we wanted to have another cat around. Of course we did but in a perhaps silly gesture to not get too involved, we never gave it a name. Instead, we always referred to it (or her to be exact) as "the big white thing". I do not suppose the cat cared whether it had a name or not so long as it got fed.

This big white thing was not the brightest of animals. Among other things, it had this constant desire to have its furry belly rubbed. She would fling herself on the floor in front of someone – anyone – and expose the belly in anticipation of affection and tickles. When we tried to walk in the garden, it was forever offering up its belly in our path. If that did not happen, it kept following us until someone relented. Diane complained that the cat got more cuddles than she did.

Unlike Dimly, the big white thing came into the house on occasion. If not having its belly rubbed, it would sit on someone's lap and drool. It was so heavy that if it sat on my lap for too long it put my legs to sleep and I hate it when my legs fall asleep because it means they will be up all night.

Like Dimly, this cat simply disappeared one day. Whether it got sick and crawled off to die somewhere or merely went in search of better food and accommodation, we never knew. Maybe it was something we said. But it was such a strange cat – not to mention dumb and overweight – that we did not feel the same sense of loss that we did with Mum and Dimly. It would be a few years before stray cats once again began to appear in our garden.

The next one is the one that is still here. It was a small grey tabby that was very skittish. It liked to lie on the rockery under the tree but would run away if one of us appeared. It somehow survived an entire winter on its own but in the spring it saw me on the patio and did not run. I approached it very slowly, step by step, a thin slice of ham in my hand. It eventually took the ham from me then disappeared. I went back inside, pleased with my success, but Diane was very unsure about adopting yet another cat. "They end up breaking your heart," she said. I replied that I would only give it a bit of food because it looked in desperate need of some. "All right," she said, "but it's not coming in the house." Of course it eventually did and we named it Willow after one of Diane's favourite characters in *Buffy the Vampire Slayer.*

Willow

Willow, like all our cats, had a very distinctive personality. She did not seem to be very old and we got the impression she had been owned at some point – she seemed to have been "fixed" – but her behaviour was decidedly feral. She did not like being touched and to this day will not allow anyone to pick her up. It took us a long time to be able to pet her and even longer before she would deign to sit on a lap. We found ourselves wondering how good an idea it was to have her. But she proved capable of earning her keep.

In their wisdom, the local council decided to tear down an old fire station at the end of our street and to build a school there. The demolition apparently disturbed a sizeable population of mice who were soon turning up in everyone's gardens as well as a few houses. Willow turned out to be an ace mouse hunter. We lost count of how many mice she caught which she then played with before completely devouring them – although she did occasionally leave one on the patio for us. This unexpected talent made us regard Willow in an entirely new light.

Willow could never be accused of being affectionate but she did have one friend. An Italian family two doors away acquired an extremely cute black and white kitten that somehow got over the fence and began to follow Willow around. At first this seemed to annoy Willow but as the newcomer got bigger they began to play and roll about together and soon became the best of friends. Once outside, one would always go to the house of the other so they could be together. Diane absolutely adored this kitten who she called Mittens because of its white paws. It had the sweetest nature we had seen since Mum and Diane wished she could keep it. Perhaps she should have.

After a few months, we stopped seeing Mittens. Willow was restless in trying to find her friend. Diane asked the neighbour what had happened to the kitten and only got an evasive reply. If Diane missed the little furball, Willow was devastated. She stopped eating, she just curled up in a corner, and some of her fur fell out. We could not believe that a cat – who was an allegedly solitary creature – was capable of pining away like that for another one. Willow's distress made Diane feel worse. This went on for a couple of weeks. Willow eventually recovered but after that, if a new cat appeared, she became aggressive and wanted nothing to do with them.

Diane used to say: "Who would be a cat?" I have only gone on for so long about these cats because they were almost like family to us. Diane was forever addressing Willow as her "baby girl" and in talking to the cat she referred to me as its father. Silly perhaps but, as I said, we both loved cats. But that is enough about them. Diane and I loved other things too – not to mention each other.

Throughout our marriage, Diane and I were ridiculously faithful to one another. In my experience, this was unusual. I will confess to having two or three opportunities along the way and I suspect Diane had some as well but we never gave in to them. It is natural for the passion and intensity of the first days of a relationship to gradually cool and settle down. Diane and I seemed to evolve a very easy-going and comfortable sort of romance that made us both very happy. I was amazed – and grateful – that Diane did not appear to want anyone but me. It made me feel guilty when I was not as nice to her as I should have been, such as during hypos, or when I neglected her while at the computer in writing mode. But our closeness never diminished and Diane always loved a good cuddle. As we got older, we even managed to joke about our sex life or occasional lack of it. I posted a card in the kitchen that showed a pretty but slightly shocked woman saying: "Sex? I'd rather have a cup of tea!" Diane loved it.

I remember one time when Diane and her mother were having one of their typical female chats and I overheard Annie say: "I know how important sex is to you" before giving me a quick and smiling sidelong glance.

The old adage about the English and the Americans being separated by a common language is quite true. In the early days, I only occasionally required an interpreter. Years of being a dedicated Anglophile had made me familiar with some of the linguistic differences. I knew that a lorry was a truck, that the sidewalk was the pavement, that cookies were biscuits and chips were not potato chips. I even knew that our two countries had different definitions of fanny. But I still had a lot to learn.

The situation was not helped when Diane occasionally used a bit of Cockney rhyming slang. On my first visit, she several times referred to her hair as her "Barnet". I eventually learned this was rhyming slang for Barnet Fair although I was further confused because I thought Diane was saying "bonnet". She also had some bits of language that were all her own. One of Diane's little quirks was that she always said "mislike" rather than "dislike". I once asked her why she did that and only got a shrug in reply. Some of Diane's vocabulary was firmly rooted in childhood.

When she was little, Diane used to call Shredded Wheat "Waggy Wheat", a habit she never grew out of because it always got a smile or a laugh. When we were married and decided to buy some minced beef to make our own burgers, she out of the blue started to call the mince "waggy mash". Where the "mash" came from is anybody's guess but from that day on minced beef was known in our house as waggy mash.

On our first holiday with her parents, Diane and her mother talked about buying some jelly beans. I thought it odd that this American delicacy could be found in the south of France until I found out they were referred to the cheap plastic beach shoes that were in all the shops. They seemed to be a European tradition, especially for wading in places where there might be sea urchins and for not burning feet on hot sand. I assumed they were called jelly beans because of their bright colours.

The bed was known as the pit. A few Americanisms also found their way into our daily lives. In the early years, our accents provided much amusement as we each tried to pronounce words from the other's language. No one could say "hot dog" quite like Diane and she always laughed at my attempts to use English swear words. Diane was disappointed that my American accent faded somewhat over the course of time but I absolutely loved the way Diane expressed herself – most of the time.

There was a famous and incredibly stupid quote from an equally stupid book and movie of the 1970s: "Love means never having to say you're sorry." Well, the exact opposite is true. One of the most important – and hardest – things to say to someone you love is "I'm sorry". I have no idea how many times Diane and I apologised to one another over the years for everything from burping to letting the other down in some way. I suppose it was a measure of our love that we were able to do so and yet I feel I probably did not say "I'm sorry" enough.

Quick change of subject...

Diane was what was known as an avid reader. She loved books and was seldom without one, including and especially in the bathroom. Her tastes were varied – she told me she would read just about anything so long as it was well written – but most of her books were science fiction or stories about vampires and the occult. These had a tendency to give her very strange dreams, especially when her blood sugar was low.

When I first met Diane, her favourite author was Douglas Adams whose books she read and re-read with great delight. Unfortunately, Adams was a bit of a lazy writer and his output was limited. He compounded this shortcoming by dying young. He is buried in the famous Highgate Cemetery in London where his fans continue to stick ballpoint pens into the ground of his grave. Diane was saddened by his passing but she had already found a replacement or, more accurately, I found one for her.

I had been wandering around a large bookstore in London and found myself in the fantasy section, not my usual area. My attention was drawn to a couple of paperbacks because of their rather cartoonish cover illustrations so I picked them up and looked over the blurbs. The books were by Terry Pratchett who, at this time, had only published two or three novels. His books seemed to parody the usual fantasy stuff as he told his stories with a very offbeat sense of humour that I suspected would appeal to Diane. So I bought the two books and took them home as a little surprise present for her. Diane thought the books were fantastic and went through them at an astonishing rate. Then she immediately re-read them. This was the beginning of her lifelong love affair with the works of Terry Pratchett, which almost made me jealous.

Diane would end up reading everything Pratchett wrote, even a couple of his books for children. She eagerly awaited every new release and would be spellbound with each one. At the same time, Pratchett was becoming one of Britain's most popular authors. He was no doubt amused by the statistic that stated that his books were the ones that were most frequently shoplifted from bookstores. He was Diane's new hero.

One of her previous heroes was Bob Geldof who was the driving force behind the Band Aid record (of course they didn't know it was Christmas in Africa – few of them were Christians) and the subsequent Live Aid concert. My years in the record business had made me cynical about such events. Yes, the singers and bands were selflessly donating their time and music but the resulting exposure led to massive sales of their albums. Diane even coaxed me into doing a fun run to raise money for The Cause. But despite all the efforts, they never really had much of an impact in Africa. So I was glad that Diane's new hero was less serious and capable of making her smile and even laugh out loud.

While Diane read books by other authors – her mother introduced her to the works of Diana Gabaldon which was a real change of pace with much thicker books – she never stopped reading and re-reading Pratchett until the books fell apart and had to be replaced. One remedy for this was to buy hardback copies as the new titles came out. Diane tried to get them on the day of release and was soon lost in Discworld.

Terry Pratchett

Pratchett was the same age as me with a beard, glasses and a penchant for hats but not as tall. He was also amazing prolific but then he did not have to go to a boring office job – he just had to write. Diane completely lost herself in his books and talked about them all the time. I always said that Diane could quote lines from Pratchett books the way other people quote Shakespeare or the Bible. She talked about his characters as though they were real and had several favourites including a rather comic version of Death.

One character in particular caught her fancy. This was the Librarian who had been turned into an orangutan so that he could reach higher shelves with his long arms and whose vocabulary was limited to "Ook!" It was probably because of this character that Pratchett developed an interest in the survival of real orangutans in the wild and even went to Borneo to see them for himself. His fascination with the creatures was soon shared by Diane who got books about them, watched every television program about them, and was absolutely mesmerised by a large male orangutan we saw at the Artis Zoo in Amsterdam where they made long eye contact.

I was so amused by this new obsession that I bought Diane a twelve inch tall stuffed animal version of an orangutan that had a big smile and was holding a banana. Well, she didn't have a teddy bear. Diane liked this furry friend so much that she decided to buy one for her mother. But, to our surprise, the orangutan was promptly taken over by Ron who, Annie said, had never been allowed such toys as a child. Ron named it Spikey and kept it near him in the house. He carried it up to the bedroom at night and brought it back out again to sit on the kitchen counter in the morning. He also talked to it. Diane and I was amazed by this new side of her father and wondered why the fur on Spikey was much more worn than that on Diane's nameless twin. Terry Pratchett had a lot to answer for.

Pratchett was famous for the number of book signing sessions he attended. It was joked that the really rare copies of his books were the ones he did not sign. When he had a new book come out, he frequently had a signing session at a small bookshop in the City but Diane never seemed able to go to one. So I went instead and got him to do a special inscription for Diane which actually got a laugh out of him.

MEN AT ARMS

Terry Pratchett

To Diane
The psycho-bitch
from Hell...
(he made me write this).

Boo!

VICTOR GOLLANCZ
LONDON

Diane treasured the autograph. We eventually removed it from the book, framed it and hung it on the wall in the bedroom. Terry Pratchett was eventually knighted but he also contracted a slow-acting form of Alzheimer's which he called the "encumbrance" (I am not suggesting the two were somehow connected). He continued to write with the aid of an assistant as the condition deteriorated. He finally died in 2015, aged 66, with his family around him and his cat asleep on the bed. Many people assumed it was an assisted suicide – something he had supported – but that was never officially pursued. When Diane heard the news she cried as if she had lost a family member. Somebody said "No more Terry Pratchett" to which we could only add: "No more Terry Pratchett books." It was a very sad loss and I will never understand why J.K. Rowling was more popular than Terry Pratchett. Diane tried one of her books but gave up on it.

Diane not only shared Terry Pratchett's sense of humour but also his views on religion which were basically negative or at best apathetic. Diane never claimed to be an agnostic or an atheist – she simply wanted to be left alone to enjoy whatever spirituality she felt around her. One of her frequent expressions was "thank the gods" and I think she had a kind of affinity with old style paganism and being a part of nature. I used to tease her that if she ever became seriously ill I would fetch a Catholic priest to baptize her but she never found that funny.

Whatever beliefs Diane may have had, they were deeply personal and my darling little wife preferred to keep them to herself.

====================================

ELEVEN – NEIGHBOURS AND HEALTH

Like every married couple – and even couples who just live together – we had an occasional crisis. One of these occurred in 1991 when we came home from work to discover that our house had been broken into. The culprits had gained entry by kicking in a wooden panel beside the front door and squeezing through. Of course, our neighbours heard nothing.

The house was a mess. Nothing else was actually broken but there were things scattered about everywhere with most of the drawers emptied onto the floor. The big things like the television and the VCR were still there – it seemed that only smaller, easy to carry items were taken. However, our spare keys were missing which suggested a possible return and the immediate need for a locksmith. Diane always seems to be calm and sensible in these types of situations, told me not to touch anything and rang for the police. They carried out their usual investigation and also contacted a reliable locksmith who arrived while they were still there. They recommended a mate who not only replaced the wooden panel but installed an iron grill behind it and the one on the other side of the door to prevent the same thing happening again.

Once they had all done their thing, we were left alone with the mess. The floors were so covered that it was difficult to move around – it looked like Jackie's. Even so, it was getting late and we were tired and a little bit shocked. Diane said all we needed to do was sort out enough space to have dinner and to go to bed. The rest could wait until morning which was a Friday on which we would not be going to work.

We took our time sorting things out and returning them to their proper place while also making a list of what was missing for the insurance company. They seem to have helped themselves to a holdall and filled it with bits of jewellery, a wallet full of foreign money, assorted knickknacks, a radio/cassette player, my camera and binoculars and, very strangely, a couple pairs of our old eyeglasses. Important documents like our passports appeared untouched and, luckily, they left Diane's diabetic stuff alone. I had my credit cards with me so they were safe. In the end, it was not as bad as it might have been. The worst part was the feeling of being invaded and violated. We felt uneasy when we returned to work and when we went on holiday a couple of months later, I think I wondered every day if the house was all right.

It seems that our area was particularly prone to burglaries with many houses around us also being victims. Among these was our wonderful neighbour Fuckface who claimed to have been broken into more than once. On one occasion, a policeman knocked on our door to ask if we had heard anything or seen anything suspicious. He mentioned some of the extravagant claims F-F was making including gold and large amounts of cash which made us suspect it was really just an insurance scam. "They didn't take his Picasso?" I asked innocently.

We eventually got a few of our smaller stolen items back when the police raided the nearby flat of a known junkie and found a large collection of loot from numerous burglaries. I hoped this repeat offender was given a stiff sentence but, knowing the leniency of the courts, he probably got off fairly lightly.

Another minor catastrophe was when our monster of a boiler, which was always troublesome, finally gave up the ghost in spectacular fashion. Unfortunately, this was in mid-December and British Gas was unable to install a new boiler until the beginning of January. So we spent the holidays relying on several electric heaters for warmth and boiling water for washing. At least it gave us an excuse, as if we needed one, to huddle close together under the covers.

In between things like this, we had our ongoing war with our wonderful neighbours. Fuckface had apparently lived in his house since the 1950s and regarded himself as some sort of chief of the neighbourhood. When he needed a favour from someone, he did not ask politely but usually began by saying: "You have to..." which did not go down well with us. He thought that he knew everything and this included endless home improvement projects and his obsession with gardening. F-F had a small, oddly-shaped back garden that was the result of being on the bend of the road and having a large garage. This did not prevent him, once he retired, from spending all day every day fussing about with his plants and flowers and cutting his grass to within an inch of its life. Anyone who visited him had an obligatory tour of his domain. We were in our garden one afternoon when we heard him showing someone around. The female guest said politely "That's nice" to which Fuckface replied in his booming voice: "Yes, it is magnificent, isn't it?"

Relations were not helped by additions to his household of one of his daughters, who we called Fatty, and an emaciated relation we called the Skull, each of whom came with a pair of children who all seemed to have different ethnic fathers. The noisy kids were bad enough (one day we were in our dining room when we heard one of the mothers screaming: "Stop swinging on the light!" which gave us a hilarious mental image) but their single parents had a habit of playing extremely loud music whenever the older folks were out. It took the intervention of the council to sort that out.

In the end, we put up sturdy six foot wooden fences between us and were advised by both police and our solicitor to avoid direct contact. Eventually, the two younger women and their brats moved on and F-F and Butch began to go back to South Africa for the winter leaving their precious palace in the hands of a succession of house sitters, some quieter than others.

We knew that the empty house on the other side would not stay empty for long. It was eventually sold to an Asian developer (the type who was becoming the usual buyers in the area) who gutted the place and more or less rebuilt the inside, which was fun to live next door to. They also cleared out the jungle of the back garden, demolishing the fence in the process so that we had to have another wooden fence installed as a barrier.

The house was then rented to a family of immigrants of indeterminate origin. It was a couple with two small children but they seemed to have quite a lot of visitors including regular ones from France. The husband did not seem to be employed yet they had three cars – including a shiny BMW that sat permanently in front of the house and was seldom moved – and plenty of new appliances and gadgets. The wife was forever screaming at the kids which earned her the nickname of the Virago. She was forever cooking onions and curries at all times of the day and night, leaving her back door open so that the stifling aromas were allowed to drift our way. "Onion alert" Diane would announce as she closed the windows and lit some incense.

Of course, these were the sort who liked to pretend that they could not understand English when it was convenient for them. Even so, they managed to become friendly with F-F and Butch. Diane loved our house and garden and often said that she wished it could be magically transported, preferably to a warm climate, where they were no neighbours.

We learned to live with these domestic irritants and did our best to ignore them. But it was not so easy to ignore the health problems that poor Diane seemed to be constantly plagued with. I never really needed a doctor and I used to say that Diane used the NHS enough for both of us.

One of her simpler problems was flu which working in offices and commuting on trains was easy to catch. Once Diane had flu, it was not easy for her to shake it. Eventually, the annual flu jab would help – although a couple of times it badly affected her sugar balance – but in the meantime she needed antibiotics to get through it. This meant getting a prescription from the GP. One time the doctor, somewhat reluctantly, gave her a prescription but said: "Don't take them for a few days – see what happens." We found out that these same antibiotics were available over the counter in pharmacies in France and Spain so when we went on holiday we stocked up and Diane was ready for the next dose of flu.

During one of Diane's check-ups at Moorfields Eye Hospital, it was decided that she needed just a little bit of additional laser treatment. I was unable to go in the room with Diane to hold her hand. She told me that as she sat anxiously squirming in the chair in anticipation, the fairly young doctor asked the nurse: "How do you turn this thing on?" Diane wanted to make a break for it. Luckily, she never needed any laser treatment after that (although she would have to have cataracts removed much later) and the local health trust opened a diabetic eye screening clinic in Ilford which made the check-ups more convenient.

A more serious cause for concern was when Diane developed Ménière's disease which affected her inner ears and caused dizziness and vomiting – not a good combination. It was not a constant condition but came in attacks that could last for several hours. A couple of times I was called at work to go to Diane's office to help her get home in a taxi provided by her firm. It was a long and uncomfortable ride and on one occasion Diane was constantly throwing up into a plastic bag – but still wanting a cigarette. She was not the driver's favourite passenger.

The condition was brought under control by medication and seemed to go away altogether, although it probably affected her hearing. It certainly scared the hell out of both of us.

We went through a number of health issues with Diane over the years, some of which were directly or indirectly related to diabetes. She generally got through these episodes with sighs, some impatience and the eternal question: "Why me?" At one point it was determined that she was a bit anaemic and it was decided that the best solution was for her to have regular injections of B12. She got these every ten weeks and actually did not mind them. We could always tell when she was getting near to the end of the ten weeks because she became visibly rundown. But once she had the shot, she bounced right back and was her familiar lovable self again.

There was also a vast improvement in blood sugar tests which could not be carried out on a small battery-operated monitor that produced more or less accurate results in seconds and even stored previous tests for comparison. All that was needed was a drop of blood on a stick to be inserted. The monitors proved so reliable that Diane sometimes did six or seven tests a day to keep control of her sugar. They were also handy for settling arguments. If I felt her sugar was going low and Diane disagreed with me, I could usually persuade her to do a test in which, she was often shocked to discover that I was right.

I had become something of an expert in dealing with Diane's hypos and near misses and I eventually learned that the quickest way to bring her sugar levels up was with liquids rather than solid food. This began with orange juice but Diane came to prefer room temperature Coca-Cola. I kept a supply of straws for when her coordination was not so good. If I was unable to get her to drink, there were tubes of glucose gel which I tried, sometimes with difficulty, to squeeze into her mouth. Diane hated the taste of that stuff and always resisted it but I had been told that even if I just got some into her mouth, her gums would absorb it and bring her around. We later found little bottles of berry-flavoured glucose juice that Diane much preferred and would usually drink with no problem.

When Diane's blood sugar was low, she could be very unpredictable. Sometimes she could be violent, other times seem stoned, still other times she was funny. I would usually talk to her and ask her questions to see how aware she was. One memorable exchange was:

"Do you know what's happening?"
"No."
"Do you know who I am?"
"No."
"Do you know who you are?"
"Yes."
"Who are you?"
(big goofy smile) "I'm me!"

It is not easy to be angry with someone who has had so many ups and downs yet still had a very pleasant nature. Diane had a fond ambition of becoming a very English eccentric like Maggie Smith or Joyce Grenfell or even her own beloved Aunt Connie. I told her I was going to be a grumpy old man and her usual reply was: "Going to be?"

Over the years, I had a number of pet nicknames for Diane – some more personal than others – but the one that she liked the best was DiDiYumYum. She often referred to herself as DiDi (and once told a solicitor who called her Di that the only people allowed to do that were her mother and those she had slept with) and thought it very funny that a character in *The Mikado* was called Yum Yum so I put the two together. She used to call me silly names as well but then I found out that certain members of her family had referred to me – affectionately I hope – as The Mad Yank. So now you know the origin of this book's title.

==

TWELVE - HAMPSHIRE

Life with Diane was fun – most of the time (there are always exceptions to sweeping statements). She was warm, quirky, and sometimes silly with a laugh that ranged from a girlish giggle to filthy guffaw. She was also quiet, thoughtful and caring with a strong sense of values and the most genuine person I ever knew. She was very good at cheering me up when I needed it. Lightening one of her moods was not quite as easy but I had a secret weapon that never failed – she was extremely ticklish. A couple of months before we were married, when I was still in Baltimore, I found a book that I just had to send to her. It was called *Small Breasted Women Have Big Hearts* (I remember the cashier nodding in agreement). Diane must have liked it because she kept the book in a drawer with other personal things.

Diane told me several times that she had always wanted to have a brother and that I was the closest she ever came. That seemed very nice but also a bit worrying until she assured me that my being like a brother was only one part of our relationship.

I confess to having inherited my father's quick temper although my anger was not particularly violent and could be directed at situations as well as individuals. I tried very hard to control this impulse. I am ashamed to admit that poor little Diane was on the receiving end of an outburst on occasion for which I usually felt immediately guilty. After one such episode she told me that I scared her which was probably the worst thing she ever said to me. The last thing I wanted was for her to feel in any way about me as she had about her previous partners.

Luckily, we were madly in love and had learned too much from bad experiences to make the same mistakes again. Instead, we made new mistakes but they were nowhere near as serious.

A few years after we were married, Diane's parents decided to temporarily escape from Britain and to spend their winters in the warmer climate of Spain. As soon as the weather turned chilly, they packed up their caravan and went to join a like-minded colony of Brits in a campsite in the south. Ron told me that they had wanted to do this for a long time but hesitated because of their concern for Diane. So they were very glad when I came along. At first they would travel back to Hampshire for the Christmas holidays but soon stayed and enjoyed the festive season in the sun. One year, Diane and I flew down to spend Christmas with them which was a real experience, especially for Diane who was no fan of the British climate.

THE FOUR CHANGING SEASONS OF BRITAIN.
SPRING SUMMER AUTUMN WINTER

At around this same time, there was a major change in Hampshire. Diane's sister Lynne and her husband Brian were doing well in their businesses and decided to move the family up the road about a mile to a place that would be called The Granaries. They did not exactly move into new houses but took over the outbuildings that had been part of a farm. A lot of time, energy and money went into converting an old barn into a spacious and stylish home that still retained its rustic exterior. Annie and Ron would move into a single level, L-shaped dwelling that had once been a stable. Part of this was also made into an office for the business and – just for the boys – a room with a snooker table. There was also another barn that became a storehouse for expensive and vintage cars that were part of Brian's trade and a small stable for a bewildered looking grey horse called Flint. Surrounding all this were huge fields and access was by a private road. It was all very impressive. All of Lynne and Brian's homes – and even their holiday house in France – seemed to be in the middle of nowhere and I used to jokingly ask Diane: what are they hiding from?

Annie and Ron's new home

Despite the physical distance between them, Diane had great affection for her family and tried to keep track of what was happening with them during frequent and lengthy telephone chats with her mother. Lynne's three kids – and Diane always referred to them as kids no matter how old they got – were all the nice and pleasant English children I used to see in old movies, except when the youngest, Hannah, went through her terrible teen phase. Diane seemed especially fond of Charlotte and Annie once confided that she was their favourite too. The kids responded warmly to Diane and I think she hoped they regarded her as their eccentric aunt.

The Family

When we went to Hampshire, it was primarily to see Diane's parents. Even though they lived just yards away from the Wiggins family home, we often only saw Lynne in passing or when she came in for a brief chat. Like Diane, my relationship with her sister was a changeable one, only more distant. Although I found Lynne attractive, it was difficult to warm to her. I had no relationship with her husband Brian at all. I do not think he said a total of three dozen words to me in all the time I was married to Diane. This did not seem to be because he did not like me. He was simply always busy and we had absolutely nothing in common apart from our wives being sisters – very different sisters.

In the summer of 1994, there was a huge celebration at the Granaries. That year marked Annie and Ron's fiftieth wedding anniversary, Lynne and Brian's twenty-fifth, and our tenth so it seemed there was plenty to celebrate. It was hardly a subdued affair into which Diane, as usual, completely threw herself until she dropped. Fortunately, she dropped from exhaustion and not low blood sugar. I found her cuddled up next to her friend Sue leaving me and Sue's husband, rock musician Lee Kerslake, to make our own entertainment which, thankfully, was never recorded.

Party Time!

As much as we enjoyed our getaways to Hampshire, we became more excited about our holidays to various parts of Europe. Throughout the 1990s, we evolved a pattern of having a break every three months. Because both our birthdays were in March, we would treat ourselves to a four or five day city break with our favourite destinations being Paris and Amsterdam. Proper summer holidays in the sun were in June and September and then we had the long Christmas break. This broke up our year nicely, got us away from our normal routine and gave us quality time together. In those days, holidays had to be booked through a travel agent on the High Road. Part of the fun was getting a stack of brochures and spending time deciding where to go. One year, the day after we returned from our September holiday, we went to the travel agent and made two bookings for the following year. It gave us something to look forward to.

The firms where we had the jobs we were so glad to get away from were great believers in constantly making changes so that nearly everything could remain the same. The biggest changes usually involved the coming and going of personnel. Diane's good friend Lorraine had left Norton Rose and gone to live with her husband Ron farther away in Romford. She and Diane gradually lost touch except for Christmas cards and a rare telephone call. I was always surprised at how friendships seldom seemed to be permanent with Diane.

One wonderful exception was a new workmate, a chirpy little Irish lass named Mary with whom Diane seemed to form a very close bond and about whom I was forever hearing. I sometimes encountered them during the lunch hour in a café called Chubbie's but I usually felt I was intruding on a very private, girls' only conversation. I have no idea how much Diane told Mary about her life but they seemed capable of sharing just about everything – except me, of course.

Mary Nelson

The friendship continued after Mary moved on to other jobs and a quest for a degree. In later years, after Diane and I had retired, we would meet Mary regularly. At first these get-togethers consisted of visits to museums and a lively lunch afterwards. Eventually, the three of us would simply have a long lunch in a small café in Greenwich and then go for a leisurely wander around the various sights, shops and the market. Diane really looked forward to these days with Mary. I sometimes felt a bit superfluous as the two of them endlessly chattered and giggled but I was reluctant to let Diane make that journey on her own. Besides, if I had not gone with her, I would not have seen that bright sparkle in her eyes when she was with her very special friend.

Our modest house remained an island of sanity or, at least, what passed for sanity to us. It was our own little world that we were always glad to return to. When the weather was pleasant, the garden was Diane's sanctuary. In addition to sunbathing and puttering around with plants and flowers, she used to love to sit and listen to the birds singing. Generations of blackbirds took up residence in our tree and our bird table attracted finches and tits as well as the occasional robin (the little British robins are quite different from the large American variety I had been familiar with). Robins tend to be fairly bold and one of them not only came very close to us but followed us as we strolled up the garden. The birds have now largely disappeared to due various developments around us. Some people do not value gardens the way we did.

At the risk of sounding politically incorrect, I have to state that some ethnic minorities do not appreciate British gardens. The renters next door use half of theirs as a rubbish dump and only cut the grass two or three times a year. Those who own houses see gardens as an opportunity to expand and build large extensions to their houses that stretch way into the garden. A short distance up the street, a presumably multi-generational family built an extension and kept adding to it until it took up over half the garden. Then, at the far end, they erected a pair of "sheds with beds". The small amount of space that was left was paved over so that no greenery remained. We could only wonder how many people lived in that property.

Diane and I did so much together that we did not have very many friends. We did not plan this, it just happened that way. We certainly did not seem overly popular in the neighbourhood which we attributed to our wonderful neighbour Fuckface. We once overheard him talking to some passing pedestrians about us and saying: "They're weird. You'll see when you see them – they're weird." Coming from him, we considered that a compliment. And just in case anyone should think I exaggerate what a nasty piece of work F-F was, I should mention the time when, after an argument, he planted a wooden voodoo doll with matching umbrella (apparently a symbol of death) in our front garden.

Despite everything around us, we still loved our house. We may have idly thought about moving on occasion but we never pursued it. There was also the shared daydream of selling the house and moving to France or Spain when we retired but I do not know how serious either of us was about that. For one thing, Diane would miss the NHS – and her garden.

Diane being cheeky

Every now and then I had to stop and remind myself that I was living in England but I could never forget that the reason for that was a gorgeous and occasionally silly creature named Diane.

===================================

THIRTEEN – NOT A GOOD YEAR

The Queen (bless her cotton socks) once described a particularly bad year in her life as an *annus horribilis.* We had one of those in 2001. It started well enough. We managed to get through the winter and spent a delightful five days in Amsterdam in March. Spring was in the air and, except for the occasional hypo, we were feeling good.

Everything changed in May. Diane had a bad hypo in the middle of the night and got out of bed in a disorientated state. Whether she was trying to get downstairs or go to the bathroom was unclear because she got no farther than the bedroom door where she smashed her right foot into the door frame with so much force that she broke all her toes. She was taken to the new King George Hospital where the x-ray revealed a straight line of fracture along the base of her toes. She could not stop crying for the pain.

The doctor said they had to wait until the swelling went down before putting a proper cast on her foot. In the meantime, they applied a temporary one and we had to return a few days later. I rang Diane's work to tell them what had happened and that we were unsure how long she would be off. I took a couple of days' holiday but knew that when I went back to work Diane would be unable to cope on her own at home. The reluctant solution was for her parents to pick her up after the cast had been put on and to take her to Hampshire until it was time for her next appointment. No one was happy with this but no one had a better suggestion. This would be the first time we were apart since we were married.

Diane spent ten days with Mum and Dad before being brought back for a check-up and another x-ray. This was just before a bank holiday so she would stay at home with me before returning to Hampshire the following Tuesday. I was very grateful to Annie and Ron.

It was during this weekend that I received a phone call from my brother Frank to tell me that our father had had another stroke and was in hospital. I was shocked both by the news and the use of the word "another" because that was something no one had ever previously made me aware of. Up until that point, it was my mother who had the serious health issues including breast cancer which left her helpless and depressed. Now, without my father there to look after her, they would both have to be moved into a care home with medical facilities.

I suppose both Diane and I knew our parents were getting older but did not want to face the possibility of losing them. Diane's parents were younger and still quite active. My parents always seemed old to me. When I was young, they did not resemble the sort of parents shown on television sitcoms or that other kids had. So when they got older, they really got older. Now they were being looked after and my siblings were there if needed. My main concern continued to be Diane.

She went back to Hampshire for another nine or ten days then came back to the fracture clinic to finally have her cast removed. It was still difficult for her to walk unaided. Once she was back home, we had to assess our situation. My father was responding to treatment and my son Nick was keeping me informed on that front. The immediate question was what to do about a holiday to Spain we had booked that was due to start in a week and a half. I had thought all along that we should cancel even though such a late cancellation meant there was little chance of any refund. But Diane still wanted to go. She wanted to get away and thought the warm weather would do her good. And so, though it probably seemed selfish, we went.

At the airport, we were allowed to board early and given what they called medical seats. Diane was moving slowly with the aid of a walking stick but she was nothing if not determined when she had made her mind up. As it turned out, her mobility steadily improved but she missed being on the beach because she found it difficult to walk on sand. All things considered, this rather gentle holiday was a success.

Diane and walking stick in Spain

Once we were home again, Diane remained on sick leave and was going to physio. She was looking forward to going back to work at the beginning of July when the next bit of bad news arrived in the post.

Diane received a letter from the personnel department at Norton Rose to inform her that they had received a number of complaints concerning her performance as a legal secretary and that she was suspended while they carried out an investigation. I was upstairs getting dressed when I heard Diane scream as she read the letter. When I got to her she was unable to speak and thrust the letter at me. While Diane's initial reaction was shock, mine was anger.

Diane had been at Norton Rose for over twenty years working for a number of solicitors and partners and had only had good assessments for her work. At that time her primary boss was an up and coming young solicitor named Giles Searby with whom she thought she had a good working relationship. The fact that there were no details about these alleged complaints was frustrating and we began to wonder if the time off with her injury had something to do with it. But first we both needed to calm down to decide how to deal with the situation.

There was not much we could do until we knew the exact nature of the complaints. Diane wanted to ring Norton Rose right away to demand answers but I advised her to wait a couple of days until she could speak in a calm voice without too much emotion. In the meantime, we wrote out a list of questions to ask and points to make. When Diane made the call, I listened on the extension and passed her a couple of notes to deal with the evasive replies.

The personnel manager was a humourless cow named Marie O'Donnell. She at first seemed reluctant to even talk to Diane and was not helpful in her replies. As Diane was working her way down her list of questions and demands, this woman suddenly said: "I am not prepared to continue this conversation" and hung up. We had a tiny feeling of satisfaction that we had rattled her but no useful information.

Diane said that in the months before she was off with her injury, she had heard about several older secretaries who had been with the firm for some years being pushed out in favour of younger, and presumably cheaper, models. Most of them seemed to have left without a fight and Diane, who hated confrontations, was almost inclined to do the same. But her mother and I would not let her. Little things like her reputation, pension and a possible redundancy payment were at stake plus we were furious at the unfairness of it all.

We had one bit of very good advice – if the underlings will not cooperate, go over their heads. One advantage of being in a firm for so many years was getting to know the people who mattered. The current managing partner was someone Diane knew well and always got on with. So she wrote a carefully composed private and confidential letter to him explaining her situation, the lack of any information, and asking for any help he might be able to give.

Within a few days, Diane received a marginally more polite letter from O'Donnell stating that interviews had taken place with relevant fee earners and copies of their statements were enclosed. She also said that Diane would now need to attend an interview and make a statement. She said this was not a disciplinary interview but that one might be required once all the statements had been reviewed. Diane's interview would be at the end of July.

We were now finally able to find out exactly what the complaints against Diane were. The statements were vague at best and lacking in specific details which was surprising considering the main one was written by a lawyer. Searby did not back up a single complaint with a date, time or client and made wild statements about everyone being afraid of Diane. Apparently this statement by Searby was so incomplete that he had been asked to expand on it in a second statement but it was just more of the same with a couple of digs at Diane's personality. The current trainee solicitor's statement sounded like she was embarrassed to be in the position and said next to nothing.

After reading the statements, we felt it was obvious that the issue was not Diane's performance but rather that she had been targeted – probably by a partner named Juliet in the department – for removal and Searby, like a good Nazi, was just following orders. Now we needed to prepare for Diane's interview and I felt the best way to do that was to prepare her own written statement rather than just replying to questions and probably getting emotional in the process.

I decided to combine my writing skills with the bits of legal knowledge I had acquired in my own jobs to put together a response that would tear Searby's statement to shreds and defend Diane's work ethic and record. After she made a few suggestions to my first draft, I produced a nine page statement that pointed out the lack of detail and inconsistencies in the complaints and occasionally turned defence into offence. We also mocked Searby's claim that he was sometimes afraid of Diane and wondered why he had waited until she had been on sick leave for two months to make his complaints. It was one of the better things I have ever written.

In the midst of all this, I had another phone call from my brother Frank to tell me that our mother had died. This was unexpected, at least to me, because I thought it was my father who was in a serious condition. But, apparently, being moved into the care home had only deepened my mother's depression and her health quickly declined. My father, whose health was still delicate, was not told she had gone. Soon afterwards, Frank gave me details about the funeral but I said I would not be flying back to attend. This decision obviously drew a lot of criticism from my family, especially from Brother Bob, but I felt there was no way I could possibly leave Diane at that time. She was my primary concern and, besides, I had found a new family in England who were closer to me than my old family had ever been. The best I could do was to arrange for flowers to be sent.

Diane was understandably very nervous about her approaching interview. She wanted me to go with her and I would have gladly done so but we were informed that non-members of staff were not permitted. Instead, Diane called on another old friend named Alan Sedgwick for support. He had also been at Norton Rose for many years and frequently acted as a kind of shop steward for admin personnel in these situations.

At this interview, which was taped recorded, Diane informed them that she had a prepared statement and was asked to read it. She got about as far as the second paragraph before her voice completely deserted her so the statement was read aloud by one of the people from personnel. Diane watched the faces of the interviewers and saw that they did not seem to like what they were hearing. I spent the whole time waiting outside. When Diane came out she hugged me tightly, cried a little and said she wanted to go home. Alan told me he thought it had all gone really well and Diane thanked him profusely for being there.

About a week later, Diane was asked to attend a meeting with Marie O'Donnell and informed that no further action would be taken regarding any of the complaints and that she could return to work the following Monday. Diane felt sufficiently assertive to state that she had no wish to return to the same department.

It was agreed that Diane could float initially but she soon found a spot in the property department. It was interesting to note that within a year Giles Searby left Norton Rose to join a firm in the north of England and that the partner Juliet departed soon after that. And Diane never forgave her supposed good friend Jacqui Hurtado, who was the secretarial coordinator in her old department, who did absolutely nothing to support her.

Less than a month later, two months after my mother had died, my father also passed away. This was somewhat less surprising considering his state of health and how close he and my mother had been. After a lot of thought, I again decided not to travel to Baltimore for the funeral. This does not mean I did not feel anything about the death of my parents but things were only beginning to get back to normal with Diane and me. We both chose the flowers to send. My son Nick, who made a point of looking for them, found them in the basement of the funeral home and they would have probably stayed there if he had not arranged for them to be moved to the proper place.

In a way, it was just as well I did not go there because I was spared being part of the family in-fighting that sounded like something out of an old melodrama. The main combatants were Brother Bob, who had been given power of attorney when my parents went into hospital, and Sister Kathy who was both executor and primary beneficiary of my father's will. They each accused the other of all sorts of things in a row so vindictive that they never spoke to each other again. What a happy family I came from – and left behind.

I eventually received a copy of my father's will and was amazed that such a vague document could have been produced by a real lawyer. After leaving the house and other major assets to Kathy, anything that remained was simply to be divided among the children in a "share and share alike" method that never really happened. I was surprised by the size of my parents' bank account. They could easily have sold the house and used the combined funds to move into an assisted care residence – as one of my father's sisters and her husband had done –

rather than struggling in ill health on their own. Instead, they wanted their independence and most of the money went to Kathy, the baby of the family and apparent favourite. The other thing that struck me was the unnecessarily archaic language of the will – it was like something out of the eighteenth century. It made me appreciate the plain English the solicitor had used in drawing up the wills for Diane and me.

Diane had this habit of doing things and not telling me about it until long afterwards. One instance was when we had both returned to work and she wanted to meet for lunch to make a confession. All kinds of possibilities ran – no, galloped – through my mind until we finally met. What she admitted to was both unexpected and very Diane.

Shortly after my mother passed away, when Diane was still on sick leave and I was at work, a large envelope from America came in the post. It was for me from Sister Kathy. Diane thought that it might be a good idea if she checked it out first. It was all things to do with my mother's death and funeral including photos Kathy had taken of my mother lying in her coffin. Diane, who did not shock easily, was shocked. She found the whole thing incredibly morbid and even ghoulish and decided that I should never see it. So she made a little bonfire out of it on the patio. She told that that as it burned she cried and kept saying "Sorry, Sophie". She then rang her mother and told her all about it and Annie suggested that she never tell me. But, of course, Diane could not keep such a thing from me forever – at least, I hope she didn't.

I hugged Diane, told her that she probably did the right thing and that I was not angry with her. I suppose that when Kathy did not receive a reply or acknowledgment about this macabre little package, she decided not to send a similar one after my father's funeral. But after that incident, Diane always referred to Kathy as Sister Death. (Since she never met my brothers, she had difficulty knowing which was which just by their names so Frank became The Professor and Bob was The Pope. In return I jokingly gave Lynne the nickname Sister Woman.)

The day after my father's funeral was 9/11 – the infamous attacks on the Twin Towers and Pentagon. It severely disrupted all air travel in America. Diane was working but I was home where I heard about the incident by chance and then followed the developments on television. It was almost impossible to believe it was happening. I suddenly felt very American and was angered by reports that some British Muslims were celebrating the event in the streets. Almost as bad was Tony Blair and his Labour Party government who decided it was a good day on which to bury bad news of their own. When Diane came home we continued to watch the news in a silence interrupted only by gasps. Eventually, Diane said she could not stand to see the repeated clips of planes crashing and buildings collapsing because it made her cry too much.

As this terrible year dragged on, we kept wondering – what next? There were a couple of bad hypos but that happened every year. As we got into December, we had more of an annoyance than a crisis.

We had decided that we needed a new cooker and commenced trying to find one that met our requirements: gas rather than electric, an eye level grill, and narrow enough (50mm) to fit into the slot occupied by the old one. The obvious source was Currys, the country's biggest appliance retailer. They would deliver the cooker, install it and take away the old one. A date was arranged and I took the day off work to await the delivery. They never came. After an irate phone call in which I got nothing but lame excuses, a new delivery date was agreed – same result. This time I was told that the engineer in my area who did gas installations did not work on Thursdays. So why was my delivery booked for a Thursday? "Dunno."

We cancelled the order and eventually got a new cooker in January from somewhere else but we had to pay the council to take away the old one. But at least 2001 was over.

==

FOURTEEN – EARLY RETIREMENT

Fortunately, the majority of our life together was not nearly so glum. Diane and I were more relaxed and comfortable with one another than either of us had ever been with anyone else. My most abiding memory of life with Diane is that we laughed a lot. Diane loved offbeat and slightly surreal humour. She was a big fan of the spaced-out American comedian Steven Wright who made observations such as "It's a small world, but I wouldn't want to paint it" and told stories like "I almost had a psychic girlfriend but she broke up with me before we met."

There was nothing I enjoyed more than making Diane laugh – well, almost nothing. I used to tell her all sorts of jokes to get at least a smile from her. Sometimes she would say "Oh, that's terrible" and then burst out laughing – her mother was much the same. One thing about Diane was that she did not always have a good memory for jokes. I could repeat jokes a year later and she would laugh as if she had never heard it before. She especially liked silly, even childish jokes like "What do you call a mushroom at a party? – A fungi to be with." And she loved off the wall one-liners which she never forgot, her favourite being "My favourite number of the alphabet is purple." And, of course, one of her most charming traits was that she was much better at listening to jokes than telling them. But that cute smile was evident either way.

When we settled down in the evening in front of the idiot box and there was a choice of viewing, Diane always wanted comedy – unless there was something with vampires on. Our favourite comedy series in the Eighties was the wonderfully politically incorrect 'Allo 'Allo set in a small French town during the German occupation and full of very broad humour, saucy innuendoes and outrageous accents. It was one of those television comedies that consistently made us laugh out loud. We enjoyed it so much that we even got tickets to see the taping of an episode at BBC Television Centre. We would watch it again – first on video, then on DVD – and found ourselves using several of the show's catchphrases.

The cast of 'Allo 'Allo

As the quality of British comedies declined, Diane decided that she much preferred the American variety and we bought box sets of the entire run of series such as *Seinfeld, Mad About You,* and *The Larry Sanders Show.* But it was not just sitcoms. We were both attracted to the quirkiness of *Buffy the Vampire*

Slayer (even though we were probably much older than the target audience) and other Joss Whedon shows. Eventually, much of our viewing pleasure would be all sorts of American shows which seemed to fascinate Diane. A couple of them I could have done without while with some others it was just as much fun to watch Diane's reactions as the shows themselves.

But there is more to life than television – at least, that's the rumour. While our favourite hobby was each other, we found other ways to fill our spare time. After all, passion may not completely disappear but it does have a tendency to cool down a bit over the years.

I bought an electronic keyboard and a stack of music books and passed many hours playing old Broadway and movie music, 60s and 70s rock, and even some simplified classics. I may not have been a great musician but I found that playing the keyboard was a wonderful way to relax down after a day of working and commuting. It was certainly more fun than doing household chores. Diane could never understand the male philosophy about home maintenance. If a man says he is going to fix something, he will fix it. It is not necessary to remind him about it every six months.

Diane preferred gardening and reading and then reading in the garden. She was a big fan of crossword puzzles and use to buy monthly magazines of them. Sometimes when she was with her mother, the two of them worked on crosswords together – even occasionally over the phone. A running gag came out of this. When they came across a long word they could not figure out, they would ask me for help. I always told them the answer was "prostitute" and they replied by saying how terrible I was.

I may have been bad but my darling wife was living proof that the first seventy years of childhood were the worst.

Diane had always had a great interest in art (her favourite artist was Salvador Dali which should tell you a lot about Diane) and this sometimes extended beyond visits to museums to doing a bit of art herself, usually drawings with coloured pencils. Like me with my writing, she could only draw when in the proper mood. Some of her work was vaguely impressionistic or even abstract. I could never understand modern art. One especially pretentious critic had his own description of modern art when he wrote: "What you see is what you see." I preferred to think of it as what I didn't see. But Diane also tried her hand at more realistic subjects. She drew a copy of a very nice and somewhat innocent nude which we both liked well enough to frame and hang in the den. On another occasion, she took some of her pencils and a pad with her on holiday and did a drawing of me at a slight distance sitting on some rocks. It was one of the nicest things she had ever done for me.

David in Fuerteventura by Diane – 1999

Any disruption to our relative happiness and tranquillity was almost always the result of outside influences. I am not saying Diane and I never quarrelled – what couple does not – but she had made it a rule very early in our relationship that we never went to bed angry. One thing Diane could not stand was sulking which she usually dismissed as "sulk and pepper." But, unfortunately, our little existence was right in the middle of The Real World which we could dislike but not ignore.

A large part of our reality was our jobs. Diane had survived the attempt to get rid of her but she was never very happy there after that. Meanwhile my latest job, which had started out so promising, was in decline after a wholesale change in admin policies. As the centuries changed, City firms were in a rush to modernise and streamline. When Diane started work as a legal secretary, her main tool was a bulky manual typewriter. Then the typewriter became electric, changed into a word processor and finally emerged as a computer. Diane not only kept pace with these changes in technology, she enjoyed them. She was so good with a computer that she was designated a "super user" who could help others who ran into problems. She was less pleased with changing hours and when the decision was made to change secretaries from working for specific fee earners to operating in a secretarial pool.

The big legal firms, who had undergone rapid growth in the boom times of the Eighties and Nineties, were now becoming increasingly international. While most had always had token offices in places like New York, Paris and Frankfurt, now they were going global which meant they needed to function on a virtual twenty-four hour basis. They all underwent extensive re-branding to jazz up their images and some even merged with foreign law firms. In most firms, the running of the admin departments was overseen by accountants rather than managers and the bottom line became all-important. Whenever budgets needed to be trimmed, the support staff was the first target. Long service and experience were a lower priority than cutting costs.

It was in this climate in 2003 that Norton Rose decided it had more secretaries than it needed. There were several waves of redundancies and finally Diane, who was increasingly fed up with the place, took a voluntary redundancy and left the firm where she had worked for twenty-five years – but she left on her own terms. Because of all her years there, she received a sizeable redundancy package plus her full pension with the firm was intact. In the end, I doubt that she shed a single tear.

Diane was well aware that finding a new job at her age would be difficult if not impossible. Few employers were interested in people over fifty or, in some cases, even forty no matter how qualified or experienced they were. So she decided to go to various employment agencies and register as being available for temporary work. Some of the agencies were slightly encouraging while others openly sighed when they looked at her date of birth. As it happened, she was lucky – or perhaps we should say unlucky – to be offered a job at a small firm of solicitors in Stratford called Bowlings where she stayed for nearly two years.

Most of the people at Bowlings were Asian and Diane worked for a demanding little Indian woman named Johti who seemed to regard a secretary as a servant. Diane said the workload was never less than heavy and that one time Johti had berated her for not taking a phone call. When Diane explained that she had been in the loo, Johti told her that in future she should take her wireless phone with her. I have no idea why Diane stuck with that job as long as she did. The crunch came when the office manager told her she could not have time off for a break in Amsterdam. Diane left the office and never went back.

Diane managed to get a few temporary jobs with weeks of inactivity in between. The last one was not far away in Ilford at another small legal firm. Permanent staff in such places always looked down on temporary workers. One of the secretaries actually complained to the boss about Diane's perfume. It was at this point that my sweet and gentle little wife finally said: "Stuff it!"

My own work situation was also far from happy under a new management team that seemed to be invisible. I had not had an annual assessment for three years but someone decided to re-define my job into something that I regarded as a demotion. So I handed in my resignation. By the end of 2005, both Diane and I were unemployed and, to all intents and purposes, retired even though Diane was only 55 and I was 57. It seemed risky but necessary to preserve our sanity.

As it turned out, we left at a good time. In just a couple of years, the recession hit and the City firms became even more ruthless in cutting back, getting rid of people on all levels from the mail room up to partners who were perceived to be not pulling their weight. The scramble for the newly unemployed was intense and complicated by the philosophy of why hire the people who were considered superfluous by their old firms. It was not a good time to be in the City. We could feel relieved and slightly smug while following all of this on the news but we still needed something to keep us going until all our pensions kicked in.

For a few years, I had been selling some of my old stuff on eBay and Amazon, partly to make some extra cash but mostly to de-clutter the house whose pockets of untidiness were contrary to Diane's nature. I had begun by selling almost my entire collection of videos just before they were superseded by DVDs. I also unloaded a number of books through Amazon. Amazingly, I managed to do all this on my computer at work but now we had a computer of our own and I thought there was a small business possibility here. While we could still get rid of some of our unwanted junk, some quick research revealed there were some wholesale companies who specialised in providing product to small independent sellers. Diane was intrigued by this and was soon absorbed in the extensive listings of one such wholesaler.

I should point out that this was in the days when eBay was still fun and quirky and the marketplace seemed to primarily consist of individuals either with the same idea or wanting to clear all sorts of stuff out of their house. The site had not yet become the domain of established businesses and pirates from China. Similarly, Amazon was still relatively new and not yet the monster it would become.

Diane was actually excited about this change in career while I was ready to put all my old retail experience to work. First we had to decide what sort of things we wanted to sell. We did not want anything too expensive that would be easy to pack and safe to entrust to Royal Mail. For Diane, this was fun.

I had originally thought that we would sell everything under my existing eBay identity of Cowboy Buddha but Diane decided she wanted a separate account of her own which would be called, with great originality, Cowgirl Buddha. While I would continue to concentrate on DVDs, books and some seemingly masculine stuff, Diane would be listing feminine products with a decidedly bohemian and New Age touch. By the time we finished, we had a combined total of over 8500 positive feedbacks.

We eventually became customers of half a dozen wholesalers with a nice range of items. We soon found out what sold and what did not and before placing an order we would check on eBay to make sure there was not too much competition for the same stuff. Diane gradually narrowed her fairly wide range of stock down to the items that were proving to be most popular. Some of these took us by surprise. For example, she started with just a few dream catchers but was soon buying them in dozens in various colours and sizes – all of which sold quickly. She dabbled in bits of jewellery such as anklets and exotic Indian-styled earrings. One of our suppliers had wooden boxes, some decorated with Chinese dragons, others with Celtic designs. Then there were little figurines of fairies, angels, wizards and witches, a couple of which she kept for herself.

Diane decided to try selling a few candles and ended up buying them in bulk. This started with scented tea lights in various colours and aromas including black opium-scented ones. Among the most popular were Weeping Rose candles – ten inch black candles that dripped red wax when lit. But the biggest seller of all was a small wooden tea light holder in the shape of a sleeping cat. No matter how many of these we bought, they never stayed in stock for long – and Diane always supplied them with a candle which many other sellers did not.

When we started, we agreed that if we were going to do this thing, we were going to be serious about it. Our home would also be our warehouse. Large cardboard boxes filled with stock would take up space in the sitting room. The dining room table was our shipping department. We bought padded mailing envelopes by the box in assorted sizes as well as heavy brown wrapping paper and large rolls of bubble wrap. There was also plenty of heavy packing tape and labels marked "Fragile" and "Handle with Care". We had a quantity of return address labels as well as business cards to include with each shipment. For our business tagline, we borrowed one from the undertaker in *'Allo 'Allo* – "swiftly and with style".

Packing things up would be Diane's department. Being Diane, she threw herself into this by not only packing the items carefully but by wrapping each one in coloured tissue paper and ribbon like a present. I told her this was not necessary and not expected but she insisted on adding her little personal touch which she was convinced helped us to stand out.

One of the first things we sold was a tin ashtray with a picture of Jesus on the inside. This was part of our de-clutter stuff. I had bought it as a joke for Diane and, after getting the hoped for reaction, it was gathering dust on a shelf. We were amazed when it was bought by a vicar who left us one of the best feedbacks: "Holy smoke – happy vicar – fan queue!" As I said, eBay was fun in those days.

It was always a busy day when we received a shipment of new product, usually in one or two very large boxes. First we had to unpack and check everything out. Every now and then there was a breakage that we would have to get a refund for. The next step was to photograph everything for the listings. Our main kitchen counter became our studio. We propped up an old drawing board and Diane had obtained several large cotton cloths of different colours to provide backdrops. Some of the items were very small but my digital camera (a Christmas present from Diane) had a very efficient zoom function that was able to photograph just about anything sharply. Once this was done and everything was safely stored away, we decided on the prices we would charge and I took my place in front of the desktop to do all the listings. On average, we had about a hundred items listed for sale at any one time. We sold everything on a "buy it now" basis rather than messing about with auctions.

From then on, it was not unusual to log on and find messages that we had sold stuff and that payments had been made. This could happen at any time of the day or night. I remember one time it was after midnight and we were going to bed when I decided to have a quick check. We had made three sales while we were downstairs watching an old movie. Most people paid right away through Paypal. There were a few awkward buyers but that was to be expected in any kind of retail. The old saying was: you can never choose your relatives or your customers. We also sold a few things on Amazon – mostly films and books – but not too much because The Big River tended to charge more in fees.

Diane was not only happy with this change of lifestyle but also with the fact that we were working together and I also enjoyed this shared activity. We were not making a lot of money but we were getting by.

I can now confess that we never paid any tax on this income.

Diane enjoyed this retail experience so much that a few years later she decided to volunteer to work at the Cancer Research charity shop in Ilford. She also enjoyed this and it had the added advantage of meeting new people. The other volunteers were generally nice but the customers were a real mixed bag. These sorts of shops with their low level of security were easy targets for shoplifters, especially gypsies who were quite brazen and, when caught or challenged, would place a curse on everyone in sight.

The only paid member of staff was the manager, a diminutive Filipino lady named Tess. She quickly saw that Diane, who was younger than most of the other volunteers, seemed to know what she was doing and took advantage of Diane's seeming inability to say "no". What was supposed to be just a couple of hours a day twice a week nearly turned into a full time job. This took a lot out of Diane who frequently returned home late and on the verge of a hypo. There was some friction between us as I tried to convince her to cut back on this new commitment. She promised to do so but once back in the shop she was usually there until closing time. Then, after a couple of really bad hypos in the evening in the same week, Diane finally realised what was happening to her. She gradually reduced her days and hours at the shop until – very reluctantly – she stopped going in altogether. She occasionally thought about going back but her next injury made that impossible.

By this time, we were winding down our online selling business. Things were changing. Fees kept increasing as did postal costs. Royal Mail re-vamped their rates for parcels to the extent that the postage for a cat tea light holder was over twice what it had been previously. eBay made a ridiculous change to their feedback system. Buyers could still leave positive, neutral or negative feedback for sellers but sellers could only leave positive ones for buyers including non-payers or those who made false claims about non-receipt. This latter problem got to be so bad that everything had to be sent recorded – another added expense. The whole thing just was not as much fun anymore.

We stopped buying new stock and tried to sell what we still had. The few things that were left over Diane donated to the charity shop.

Our income was now dependant on pensions. Diane and I both received work pensions from our previous employers. Now Diane was able to claim her state pension. She was one of the last women aged sixty to qualify as her birthday was just a week before the cut-off date that raised the minimum age. It made me decide to investigate if I qualified for any American social security. My work life had been virtually split between the UK and the USA. I found out that the retirement had been raised to sixty-seven but that at sixty-two I could take a pension of about three-quarters what the full pension would be. I figured it was better to have the money then rather than later.

When I was sorting things out with a nice man from the embassy, he rather casually mentioned that my wife would be eligible for a spouse's pension when she turned sixty-two. My initial thought was that he did not realise that Diane was British. But, sure enough, when we contacted the embassy again, they confirmed that was the case. Diane had a semi-formal telephone interview then we went to the embassy where another very nice man issued her with a Social Security card and arranged a pension for her that was roughly half of mine – even though she had never lived or worked in America. The monthly amount fluctuated according to the exchange rate but we never complained about that – plus it increased every year.

The next thing was our mortgage. The fiasco that was an endowment mortgage meant that after twenty-five years we still owed a fair amount. Diane had put aside money from her redundancy for this but it was not enough. Then I realised that I had a second pension from Linklaters – or, rather, had stupidly thought it was part of the first one. One phone call later brought me a lump sum – most of which paid off the mortgage – followed by a modest monthly payment.

We ended up with a total of seven pensions between us and, once the mortgage was paid off, were better off than we had been when we were working. As our income usually exceeded our outgoings, Diane began to say "We've got to spend some of this money" which was a totally new philosophy for her.

===

FIFTEEN – FRANCE, BROKEN BONES, TRAGEDY

I think Diane and I both agreed with the fridge magnet that said: If I knew I was going to live this long, I would have taken better care of myself.

One of the drawbacks of being retired is never having a day off and every day being much the same to the extent that we needed to check the calendar to see what day of the week it was. Fortunately, our little business enterprise initially kept us busy so that we did not drive one another crazy. And even though we were no longer officially employed, we still managed to have a few more holidays in the sun.

These were in a quiet corner of the Spanish resort of Cambrils in a place called, appropriately enough, Cambrils Park which at that time was primarily a campsite for caravans but also offered a few rather nice two bedroom bungalows with air conditioning. These were relaxation holidays rather than adventure ones. The bungalows came complete with a bit of lawn and sun loungers and Diane had her choice of two sizeable swimming pools. It was a short walk down to the seafront with its promenade and shops. When we felt energetic we could hire bicycles or a pedalo or enjoy a round of mini-golf in which we never bothered to keep score (but we all know who won, don't we?). It was a perfect place to get away from it all and to completely refresh our minds and bodies. It was also only a short taxi ride from Reus Airport which only added to the convenience and lack of stress. I think we went there a total of six times, staying in a different bungalow on each occasion.

We had booked to go again in 2008 but complications arose over flights and affordability so we reluctantly cancelled. Diane was not happy and made sure everyone knew it. Her family kind of came to the rescue with the suggestion our of going with her parents for a stay at Lynne's holiday house in France. It seemed like a good idea. Instead of flying, we went by car and ferry for what turned out to be at least a twelve hour journey. Diane and I were crammed into the back seat with some luggage and provisions in Ron's new Kia which was the most uncomfortable vehicle I had ever been in. Diane must have felt nostalgic for the old Hillman, not to mention a joint.

The old French farmhouse/manor house reminded me of the Three Musketeers. It had plenty of space around it and a swimming pool. It was, of course, in the middle of nowhere. The interior had been completely re-done and felt more like a small provincial hotel than a home. In the main living room was a coffee table on which a number of magazines had been so carefully and neatly arranged that I could never resist messing them up. It was early evening when we arrived and we were all wasted. Lynne, who would be staying with us for the first few days, met us with a big smile and said she had prepared dinner for us, causing me to recall all the jokes her kids had made about her cooking. All that I remember of it is that Diane drank too much wine.

Diane and I had rooms in a different part of the house from Lynne and the parents – a pair of simply furnished bedrooms reached by a spiral staircase. At least it had its own bathroom. The first night was the worst. Both the journey and the wine caught up with Diane and she was soon throwing up in the bathroom. This created a problem because it instantly lowered her blood sugar levels. Every attempt to raise them only resulted in more vomiting until Diane was in full hypo mode. She was thrashing and cursing so much that I felt I had no option but to fetch Lynne for help. Together we tried, with limited success, to get some glucose gel into Diane who kept getting wilder and actually bit Lynne's hand. At this point, Lynne decided to ring for an ambulance.

It was a new experience to deal with a French ambulance crew and they were accompanied by a rather attractive female doctor who I tried to communicate with in broken French. They managed to restore Diane to what passed for normality and, after that, we all went to sleep. I slept very late the next day and Diane, with her usual post-hypo guilt, decided not to wake me but went grocery shopping with Lynne and their parents.

The rest of the holiday was fairly subdued, especially after Lynne left, and consisted primarily of trying to amuse ourselves around the house and the occasional shopping trip into the nearby town of Lectoure. Ron seemed to be in a permanently grumpy mood with little interest in doing much and Annie mostly stayed with him. Diane and I went for walks and played boules on the gravel driveway. The saving grace was the swimming pool which Diane was in every day and even persuaded me to have a chest-high wade or two.

I tried to convince Diane that, since we were in such a secluded place, she could swim naked as she had done on some of our previous holidays in naturist settings. But she continued to spend her time in and around the pool topless. I could only attribute this uncharacteristic modesty to the presence of her parents.

There were a couple of more minor hypos and it was then that I learned the value of orange juice to quickly bring Diane around. In a room filled with soft furnishings was a large screen television but the only thing we watched was the final of the French Open tennis tournament in which Diane's favourite Rafael Nadal beat Roger Federer. When it came time to leave, we did not feel the usual regret of a holiday ending. The journey back was even worse than before with the ferry crossing being late at night and Diane being seasick most of the way.

When we arrived in Portsmouth, there was a slight delay getting through Immigration because the officer on duty was either confused that I had an American passport but was a UK resident or he could not find the appropriate stamp to mark my arrival. I explained that although I was American, my wife was British. "Why don't you become a British citizen?" he asked to which I replied, with calm and extreme logic "Because I'm an American."

Fairly early on, after I had settled into my new life and obtained my permanent resident status, I began to wonder if I should change my citizenship. After all, I intended to live the rest of my life in the UK so perhaps I should become British. Diane offered no opinion and said the decision would have to be mine. I thought about it for a long time then filled out the necessary paperwork and sent it, along with my passport and a fee, to the Home Office. Many months went by and I began to question the wisdom of my decision. Then we were due to go on holiday to Spain and I needed my passport back. Once I safely received it, I advised the Home Office to cancel the application. I had decided to remain an American and I am very glad I did.

I was actually annoyed by the long delay in this process and could not understand the reason for it (I was still not completely accustomed to British bureaucracy). I mean, I was married to a British citizen, gainfully employed, paid taxes and made no demands on the benefits system (unlike many immigrants) – I thought they would be glad to have me. Another source of irritation was seeing the parade of athletes with very tenuous links to the UK being given immediate citizenship so they could represent the country in the Olympics, tennis, cricket or whatever. And many of these new citizens did not even bother to live in the country. So every ten years I went to the American embassy to renew my passport and was very glad to have it.

I do not think Diane had ever been so glad to get back home to Ilford. The holiday had not exactly been a disaster but the travelling left a lot to be desired. It turned out to be the last trip we ever made with Annie and Ron and they were no longer driving up from Hampshire to visit us. They were getting older and both had health problems with Annie having to be fitted with a pacemaker. If not then but soon afterwards they stopped going to Spain for the winter and the English climate could not have helped either their conditions or their moods. We still made some trips to Fordingbridge to see them and Diane and her mother had their regular marathon phone calls.

At least Diane felt close to her family. As my son Nick became more or less grown up, his visits to see me ceased. We communicated for a while through letters and occasional phone calls and then emails. Nick seemed to spend a lot of time on Facebook so I joined Facebook for a while primarily to keep up to date with what was happening with him. It was through one of his posts on Facebook in 2004 that I learned that my ex-wife Jackie had died after battling cancer for several years. I felt strangely unemotional about this news – we had been divorced longer than we were married. My contact with Nick continued to be sporadic. Diane was always sad that Nick and I did not seem to be very close and she used to encourage me to communicate more. But now Nick has a wife and son of his own and is very busy with his life. I resigned myself long ago to the fact that I was not a very good father.

My son and grandson

Diane now seemed to sometimes have periods of feeling very restless which she described as wanting something but not knowing what it was. In 2010, her mood was not helped by the ending of summer and the approach of her least favourite month of October. I was at my desk when she came into the den and sat on the bed. It was mid-morning and she had not yet had her bath which usually had a soothing effect on her. But as she talked about nothing in particular I realised that her sugar levels were on the low side. I had a glass of cola and suggested that she have a few sips. "I'm fine!" she shouted at me and I knew this was not going to be one of those times when she was nice and cooperative. The attempt to get her drink turned into an argument and she stormed off into the bathroom, slamming the door behind her. The next thing I heard was a crash.

I found her lying on the floor with one leg propped up on the side of the bath. She was crying and in a hypo. I managed to get some glucose gel into her and she slowly began to come around. As she did so, she started to cry out in pain and we both saw that her right ankle, the one on the edge of the bathtub, was red and beginning to swell. I got her back to her bed and tried to calm her down.

At first, we both assumed she had sprained her ankle and treated in accordingly with bandages. She still had the crutches from her previous injury so she was able to move around a little bit. But the pain did not subside so, after a couple of days, we went to the emergency room at King George Hospital. Of course, these things always happen on weekends so there was a wait of several hours. When she was eventually examined and x-rayed, it was discovered that she had two fractures in her ankle. The doctor said they could not treat such an injury at King George (don't ask me why) so she would be transferred to Queens Hospital in Romford. There was another lengthy wait for an ambulance to take her there and another lengthy wait to be seen by a doctor. By this time it was late at night.

The doctor wanted to keep her in overnight and operate on her in the morning by inserting pins in her ankle. Diane was strongly opposed to this because she had heard that these pins had bad effects on diabetics. All she wanted was a good cast that would allow the fractures to heal naturally. There was a long debate about this until finally the doctor had her admitted to a ward and told her to think about it and make a final decision in the morning. Leaving Diane there that night was one of the hardest things I ever had to do.

With some difficulty, I managed to get through to Diane's ward on the phone the next morning. I was told she was in the process of having a cast put on and I replied that I would be there soon to take her home. Diane told me she had a terrible night and the nurses were not particularly nice to her. The doctor was more than miffed that she refused to have the pins. All Diane wanted was to go home but the sister in charge of the ward was reluctant to release her. In the end, I got hold of a wheelchair and we more or less discharged ourselves.

At least this time I did not have to go to work and could look after Diane myself. We coped reasonably well and I actually got a laugh out of her when I told her I would everything I could for her – except wiping her bum. The stairs were the most fun. We now had two pairs of crutches so we had one upstairs and one downstairs. Diane made her way in between them one step at a time on her bottom. When she got to the top, she sat on the floor and I grabbed both her hands and pulled her up. She always thought the countdown of "one, two, three – up!" was quite funny but we were both relieved she was able to laugh at anything.

After her previous injury, I began to sleep in the den where the old sofa bed had been replaced by a proper single bed. Diane had worried that I might knock against her injury in my sleep. Because our sleeping patterns were so different (Diane liked to read in bed until the early hours) this turned into our normal arrangement. I had become a much lighter sleeper than I used to be and I developed a kind of sixth sense to be aware of Diane having a hypo during the night. As it happened, she did have one or two and it was quite a challenge to deal with someone thrashing and kicking their legs in the air when one of those legs had a plaster cast on it.

It was a long recovery with several trips to the fracture clinic at Queens and then physiotherapy at King George and sheer bloody minded determination. Diane had started off crying that she would never walk again then became impatient to do so. She went from using two crutches to one crutch to two walking sticks to one walking stick. We began by taking short and slow walks up the road. I nearly got into a fistfight one time when an idiot on a bicycle suddenly came up behind us (bikes on pavements is one of my pet hates) and came within a couple of inches of Diane. But we persevered and went just a little bit farther each time until the day Diane said she wanted to try it on her own, knowing full well I would never be very far behind.

From then on, I suggested – no, pretty much insisted – that Diane always use a walking stick when going out. I got her an adjustable one with a comfortable ergonomic handle. Of course, she was not happy about this but I said it was best to have it if only to keep her from losing her balance on the uneven pavements plus for getting a seat on the bus. She worried that she would look like an old lady and I reminded her that she was sixty. "I may be getting older," she said, "but I'm never going to be old." She maintained that attitude even when dyeing her greying hair, getting dentures and being fitted with hearing aids. All right, I was not exactly aging gracefully myself but at least I did not have all those spare parts. I was just a grumpy old man.

During the extended time that Diane was laid up with her broken ankle, she occasionally wrote down some of her stray thoughts in a notebook to help relieve her restlessness and moments of depression. These notes were mostly lamenting the pain and her lack of mobility, complaints about the difficulty in getting physio appointments, fears of not being able to walk properly again, and concerns about her mother who was having health issues of her own at that time. Once in a while, Diane was in a reflective mood. I only recently found her notebook and came across this entry:

"I've had a full life – enjoyed so much and done a lot of things other people haven't. I have been very lucky."

I could actually hear Diane's voice saying those words – they are so typical of her. Diane often made such fatalistic statements. More often than not, they were followed by a smile and a little giggle.

Time was passing – sometimes much too quickly – and we were all getting older. Diane's mother was showing early signs of a form of Alzheimer's which played havoc with her short term memory. She could clearly remember things from years ago but not in the last five minutes. She remained in a fairly cheerful but confused mood and would ask the same questions over and over. Diane was understandably distressed by all this but Ron found it difficult to cope with. He even asked me how I had managed to live with Diane's diabetes for so long but the only advice I could give was to be very patient which was never one of Ron's virtues.

Ron was having his own problems with persistent coughs and breathing difficulty. He had been a smoker. On our first holiday together in France he introduced me to the small non-filtered cigars called Café Crème which led me to change from cigarettes to cigars (which I gave up, much to Diane's astonishment, when I quit work in 2005). Once he gave up, he became intolerant of Diane's habit and she could only smoke outside when we visited them. But then Ron would spend hours sitting next to a wood burning stove which could not have helped his condition. Lynne told me much later that Ron had never entirely given up smoking and used to sneak off to quiet places for a quick fag.

Diane was sad and shaken by how much her once lively parents had changed and our visits to them became shorter and less frequent because she was so upset at seeing them. Then in 2012, Ron's condition deteriorated and he was taken into hospital. Diane and I were constantly on the phone to both Lynne and the hospital which said he was "poorly" which I found out was British for "not very well at all." Diane's impulse was to rush down to Hampshire but she was suffering from a chest infection herself and was hesitant about going into a hospital with it. But as the situation worsened, we packed some bits and got on a train. We were too late. Ron passed away while we were still on the train. We waited at the house for the return of Annie and Lynne.

*One of Diane's favourite photos of her father,
taken in France wearing my hat*

I have to admit that I had long dreaded the passing of one of Diane's parents because I knew how hard it would hit her. Now she was not only upset at his death but angry at herself – and probably me too – for missing the chance to say goodbye. But she found the strength to realise that the important thing now was for her to look after her mother. Annie was in a more confused state than ever so, while Lynne became busy making the necessary arrangements, we stayed with Annie and tried to comfort her. I doubt mother and daughter were ever closer.

It is sad to report that I was not much help. After two or three days, I was suddenly struck with a violent strain of norovirus which totally wiped me out. Everything was, as they say, coming out of both ends at a steady rate even though I found it impossible to eat anything. Where this came from we will never know but apparently I was in such a bad state that Diane was afraid she was going to lose me to. When the norovirus started to ease it was replaced by a kind of flu that left me with a persistent cough, a burst eardrum and incredible nightmares. So Diane had both me and her mother to look after but then she was always very good in a crisis, even if she did have a couple of hypos.

We had to wait two weeks for the funeral by which time I was able to move around a bit. Diane had wanted me to do a reading at the service but my cough left me with no voice so young Charlotte did it instead. Just to complicate things, Diane had a fairly bad hypo early in the morning of the funeral which exhausted me and frightened her mother. Once all that had calmed down, Diane went to help Annie get ready. She seemed more confused than normal and Diane gently told her it was time for the funeral. I shall never forget Annie's weak little voice saying: "But I thought we did that already."

The funeral was well attended and its non-religious aspect was demonstrated by playing the theme music from Ron's favourite sports shows rather than hymns. Annie clutched Diane' hand throughout and I felt sad but useless. Everyone gathered at a country pub afterwards but Annie, Diane and I did not want to be there and Charlotte kindly took us back to the house which felt very cold. Annie looked completely lost and we had very mixed feelings about leaving her and going back to Ilford – but we could not stay there forever. The journey home was uncomfortable in several ways and we knew that things would never be quite the same again. More than anything else, Diane worried about her mother.

Life must go on. What an irritating cliché that is.

Ron had passed away in November which meant that Christmas was going to be a sombre occasion that year which did not bother me too much because I was becoming a Scrooge anyway. Diane, as could be expected, was never quite the same but she managed to bounce back, at least partially, better than I could have hoped. The tiny silver lining in the great dark cloud was that we still had each other.

===

SIXTEEN – BLOOD SUGAR LEVELS

When I wrote the book about our holidays and adventures in various parts of Europe, Diane – who was such an avid reader – said that she felt strange being a character in a book that would be read by people she never met in addition to the expected audience of friends and family. But she was always glad to have a record of so many happy times we had spent together. It was remembering her reaction to that book that prompted me to write this one – and at this point I feel that I have merely scratched the surface of the story of our relationship.

I could write so much more about my life with Diane and there are some things I prefer to keep to myself but I think that sharing these memories and preserving them has been a good sort of therapy for me. Yes, the experience has made me realise how much I had lost – as if I could ever forget that – but it also made me feel glad that Diane and I had so much together.

A character in one of my books said: "Love is like the Loch Ness Monster. It's a charming idea to believe in but it's never there when you go looking for it." I loved that line but my own experience was quite the opposite. Diane and I were not looking for love when we started to write letters to each other – love found us.

Of course, no love story would be complete without a few complications. In our case, most of these were caused by a little thing called diabetes from which there was no escape or respite. I would hate to create the impression that diabetes was the dominant factor in our life together but it was something that was always in the back of our minds and, when it emerged, was virtually the only cause of tension between us apart from an occasional and easily forgotten marital spat. Perhaps it was because we were now retired and together all the time that low blood sugar levels seemed more of an issue. It is also possible I was being over-protective of a very independent individual.

When Diane was working as a legal secretary, she said that she survived on adrenalin, coffee and cigarettes. She always seemed to do everything in a hurry. Because she was diabetic, she had this notion that she needed to prove that she was just as good and capable as anyone else, if not better. This was a hard habit to break. When she was home, whether she was doing housework, gardening or packing up parcels, everything was done at full speed ahead. This included walking which should have been a leisure activity but in which she employed what she liked to call her "power walk". I had always been a strong walker, used to going long distances, but as I got older I found it increasingly difficult to keep up with Diane. As the distance increased between us, I would frequently call out: "I'll see you there." The amazing thing was that Diane carried out all these activities while smoking but rarely seemed to be out of breath. When I told Diane that we had reached the stage in our lives when we should be more relaxed and taking it easy, her reply was: "Why?" Oh, how I loved that woman!

All this expenditure of energy had an effect on her blood sugar levels. To my mind, if Diane was intending to engage is some sort of activity, she should stock up on the all-important carbohydrates beforehand. But Diane preferred to do things and deal with her sugar levels afterwards. For some reason I could never understand, she insisted on living on the edge.

It was easy enough to test Diane's sugar with her little monitor that she used at least six times a day. She felt this gave her better control but her monthly prescription for the necessary testing strips was not adequate for that amount and her GP would not increase it, no doubt due to budget cuts. We found we could purchase as many strips as we needed on eBay at less than half the price charged by chemists. Where the people who sold the strips got them was something we did not worry about so long as they were genuine with long expiration dates. We had enough so that any time I thought Diane's sugar was getting low and she disagreed, the question was easily solved with a quick test.

The only problem, from my point of view, was how Diane reacted to low scores on the monitor. Instead of filling up on carbohydrates, she tended to eat just enough to get her to the next test at which point the process would be repeated. I used to compare her to a car that was running out of fuel. Instead of filling up, she would just have a litre or two, get to the next filling station (blood test) and do the same – all the way until her major meal in the evening. She liked to have a fresh croissant at lunchtime but otherwise relied heavily on chocolate which was not as long lasting as things like bread or biscuits. The other standby was the berry-flavoured glucose juice. She always carried one or two of the small bottles in her bag and there were other bottles in every room in the house for a quick fix. One bottle of this berry juice could raise her sugar level and prevent a hypo in about ten minutes and, luckily, she did not argue too much about drinking it.

Everyone told Diane that she should keep her sugar levels, according to the monitor, between 6 and 8 but she seemed to think she was safe having it between 4 and 6. This left a very narrow margin of error. She kept a written record of her tests and the number of 2s and 3s was always worrying. Sometimes it was fairly apparent, even to her, when her sugar was low but other times the level dropped very quickly. It was not so bad during the day but the middle of the night was another story. That was when we usually needed an ambulance.

I always treated calling for an ambulance as a last resort, preferring to try to bring Diane out of a hypo on my own. Even though she sometimes fought with me, I knew that she would be scared enough waking from a hypo without seeing several paramedics looming over her. And we never knew what sort of ambulance crew would show up – or long they would take.

Most of the crews were fine – professional, understanding, caring – especially the females. There was one particularly kind young woman who came to us two or three times. On her last visit, when the ordeal was over, Diane took her hand and started to cry, saying in a weak voice: "You never see me when I'm nice." But some crews were curt and even aggressive and scared Diane more than the hypo had. To make matters worse, Diane's hypos became more and more violent to the point that I called for help less for the hypo but more out of fear of Diane hurting herself. One evening we were watching television when Diane suddenly "went into one" and was rolling and thrashing all over the sitting room the floor. In the end, it took three paramedics to hold her down while a fourth administered the miracle injection known as GlucaGen.

Some of the commotion caused by these hypos could obviously be heard by our neighbours because we later learned that Fuckface and Butch had told at least one other neighbour that I regularly beat my wife.

The worst episode with an ambulance crew was in late 2017 when we got a crew who had been called in from another area. They were at the end of their shift, in a hurry and seemed to regard Diane as a nuisance rather than a patient. Diane was unconscious in a really bad hypo. There are two ways for an ambulance crew to deal with this. One was an injection of GlucaGen, the other was to set up a glucose drip into her arm. This lot chose the latter but the surly woman failed to insert the line correctly so instead of the glucose going into the bloodstream it simply collected in the arm. Unfortunately, no one seemed to notice this and Diane's lack of response made them decide to take her to a hospital. The other problem was that these people chose to absolutely ignore me and at one point kept me out of the room.

The chief paramedic went to the ambulance to get the chair they used for transporting patients and told me to clear a path from the door to the stairs. While we were out of the room, the woman apparently realised her mistake and gave Diane an injection of GlucaGen. By the time the chair was brought into the room, Diane was beginning to come around. But instead of leaving her in bed to recover, they insisted on forcing her onto the hard metal chair. Again, I was kept out of the room. When I finally got back in, I found Diane in tears and both her legs covered in cuts and gashes. The crew tried to tell me that Diane had inflicted the injuries on herself to which I replied: "And you just stood there and did nothing to help her?"

Now it was necessary to take Diane to hospital not because of her hypo but because of her injuries. Again the woman was rude and in a hurry, telling Diane to put some clothes on and not giving her a chance to get her glasses, dentures or hearing aids. As I tried to gather up a few things for her such as a jacket and a box of tissues, I heard the front door slam. I looked outside and the ambulance was gone. They did not bother to wait for me or tell me where they were taking my wife.

As it turned out, they did not go to a local hospital but to one in Newham close to the crew's depot. I managed to get there and it took all of my self-control not to hit anyone, especially when the head paramedic started talking about Diane's mental state. As Diane was taken into a cubicle for the long wait to be seen, the ambulance crew disappeared.

It would take a couple of months and several trips a week to the nurse at our GP's for Diane's injuries to heal. In the meantime, I lodged a formal complaint with London Ambulance Service about the behaviour of the crew and the fact that my wife had been badly injured while supposedly in their care. After some correspondence, an investigation was launched but it was a case of the ambulance service investigating itself. This dragged on for months with numerous excuses for the delays. When a hearing was finally scheduled, it was cancelled because it was snowing that day. We were told there would be another hearing at the end of March but this date fell in the middle of a week when we would be in Paris – a much-needed break for Diane. We assumed a new date would be set but they went ahead without us – a hearing in which only one side of the story was told. The crew got off with a slap on the wrist for some of their behaviour but nothing was resolved about Diane's injuries or how she got them.

After reading the report of this hearing, we made another formal complaint to the Health Ombudsman only to find out that they nearly always took the side of the NHS. Perhaps we should have gone to a solicitor and sued for negligence but, after the ambulance service report that would probably have been impossible to prove. After that, it would take an extreme situation for me to call for an ambulance again and on the couple of occasions when I had to, Diane looked at the crew with fear in her eyes.

Both the diabetic clinic in Ilford and one of the doctors at the GP's surgery suggested that we be given a prescription for GlucaGen and that I be trained how to inject it. This would save the need for calling for an ambulance. It seemed a sensible idea and I was more than willing to give it a try. But, despite several queries, it never happened. I even looked to see if I could buy GlucaGen online. Meanwhile, Diane just wanted to get back to a normal life and promised to be a good girl. She also wondered what she could have possibly done in a previous life to have been a diabetic.

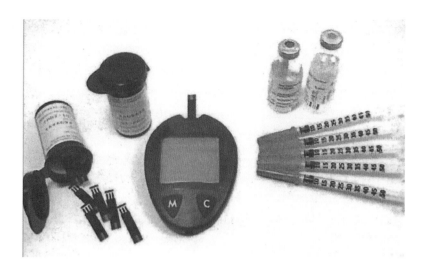

It is starting to sound like our life together was nothing but doom and gloom but it was very far from it. Diane and I were always looking for new ways to amuse ourselves and occasionally finding some. A few of these were fun while others were time-consuming matters of necessity such as having a new roof put on the house, part of the joys of owning an old place that always seemed to need something doing to it. With our online selling a thing of the past, we found other things to do, both individually and together.

When the weather was really nice – and the British summers seemed to be improving (thank you global warming) – Diane was mostly in the garden while I hid from the sun at my desk in front of the computer. When the weather was not nice, this tended to annoy Diane. While writing new books and re-writing old ones for publishing is a solitary activity, I now regret how much time I spent on it and away from Diane. It was time that could have been much better spent. Sometimes Diane would drop little hints about feeling slightly neglected and complain about getting only "crumbs of affection" – a situation which required my immediate and undivided attention.

Diane's "crumbs of affection" phrase was really just a tease. We frequently did little things to show our appreciation and feelings for one another even if it was just a silly card for no special occasion. I always had a big bouquet of flowers delivered for her birthday, our anniversary and Valentine's Day (I was never one of those husbands who forgot important dates). And on my birthday Diane...well, she was always very nice to me on my birthday.

After her various injuries, Diane kept up with some of the exercises the physios had taught her. In particular, she wanted to strengthen her legs so that she would not need a walking stick – and walking was her favourite exercise. Unless it was raining, she took a long walk to and around Valentine Park, even once on Christmas Day when she was disappointed to find the park closed. She tried to coax me into doing some exercises but I told her that I had always had plenty of exercise in jumping to conclusions, pushing my luck, and dodging responsibilities. Of course, there was also the fun of tackling the garden which seemed to get bigger every year.

Sport is a big thing in the UK but we mostly ignored it. If we came across a football match when flipping through channels, Diane immediately said "No!" When the news would announce the latest cricket score, she always said "means nothing to me." Interestingly, when I got a couple of tapes of baseball games, she found them interesting despite any resemblance to cricket which was once described as baseball on Valium. In 2019, the New York Yankees and Boston Red Sox played two games in the Olympic stadium in nearby Stratford (a venue really not designed with baseball in mind). Diane said she might like to see one of the games out of curiosity but changed her mind once we saw the ticket prices.

The one sport she did like was tennis which she would watch for hours – so long as Andy Murray was not playing. Her favourite player was Rafael Nadal – she called him her "baby" – who we first saw on Spanish television on holiday when he was still a long-haired teenager who looked like an Apache. Diane, who was famous to talking to the television ("they can't hear you" I kept telling her), always talked to Rafa who was young enough to be her son. Well, she could have had a lot worse obsessions.

Every now and then, usually during our rambling late night discussions, Diane and I would wonder how we ever managed to find one another and come together. When people asked how we met, we continued to be a little surprised ourselves that the story was so seemingly romantic. I usually tried to make a joke about it but Diane was always wistful and tender about the memory of those early days. Even so, I suspect that her earlier experiences had taught her to keep just a few very personal thoughts to herself.

I wonder what this book would be like if Diane had written it.

===

SEVENTEEN – ANOTHER TRAGEDY

Diane had a much stronger sense of family than I did. Even though there was a physical distance between her and her family, she always wanted to be closer emotionally. It was not always easy. She was determined to continue her regular phone calls to her mother even though Annie was sometimes less responsive than before. In the summer following Ron's death, we made what turned out to be our last trip to the Granaries. As usual, we went by train to Salisbury but now we had to rely on a taxi to take us the final ten miles or so to Fordingbridge.

That last visit was somewhat uncomfortable. Our relations with Lynne, who seemed somehow tense and distant, became strained. Annie now appeared frail and alternated between being quite lucid to seeming to be in her own little world. Diane wanted to be as helpful as possible but in reality there was little we could do except trying to be a loving presence. We left knowing that Annie would probably not even remember that we had been there.

Shortly afterwards, Lynne and Brian suddenly and without much warning sold the Granaries and moved to a smaller but equally secluded house on the other side of Fordingbridge, taking Annie with them. She now lived in a room with a television which must have further confused her. Before we could visit her there, she had a couple of health problems and Lynne decided it was best to move her into a care home where she could have company and support. The place was called Glynn Court and was actually just a short distance down the road from the Granaries. Diane and I remembered seeing it when we went for walks and I think I once even joked about putting Diane in there if she did not behave. Annie made the transition well and enjoyed being with people which greatly improved her general mood and outlook. She appeared to be a favourite with the staff.

Annie and Diane in happier times

Care homes are frequently referred to as "God's waiting rooms" and no doubt some are better than others. At least Glynn Court was in a peaceful rural setting and it was here that we would now visit Annie. Because the family had moved, we now stayed in a hotel in Salisbury and then travelled to Glynn Court to spend an afternoon with Annie. She was always glad to see us even though she seemed to reside in a different room nearly every time. Diane insisted on bringing flowers and chocolates and once we left the common room for Annie's own little space it was almost like old times – almost. As much as we enjoyed seeing Diane's mother, we could not deny feeling a sense of relief to escape from Glynn Court. Every time we left, Diane said to me: "Don't ever put me in a place like that."

Another change from our previous trips to Fordingbridge was that now we had a chance to spend some time in Salisbury, a very pleasant town that we had only passed through before. In addition to its magnificent cathedral and the proximity to Stonehenge, Salisbury was a relaxed change of pace for us and a good place to wander, except when Vladimir "Ras" Putin was having local residents poisoned. Terry Pratchett supposedly lived near Salisbury but we never saw him. Instead, Diane enjoyed the little shops and dining out in the evenings.

By now, Lynne's "kids" now had kids of their own and on the rare occasions when we saw them, Diane loved to make a fuss of them. Her love of children was not something I necessarily shared. She delighted in sending them money for Christmas and their birthdays and receiving little thank you notes in return. As I said, Diane had a strong sense of family.

As I indicated earlier, Diane acquired some "spare parts" as she got older, in particular dentures and hearing aids. The former proved to be quite an ordeal. The problem was loose teeth that threatened to fall out. There was nothing wrong with the teeth themselves, it was her receding gums that could barely support them. Diane liked to pretend that the problem with her gums was a side effect of diabetes but the dentist said it was the result of heavy smoking. At least we were able to find a nice Greek born woman who specialized in dealing with very nervous patients. I held Diane's hand throughout and had the imprint of her fingernails for days afterwards.

The hearing aids were easier. The difficulty there was it took years to convince that Diane that she needed them after constantly having to raise my voice to be heard ("Don't shout at me!") and needing subtitles when watching television. Her hesitancy seemed to stem from the mistaken belief that all hearing aids were the large obvious ones her father had. Once she realised that technology now produced aids that were so small they could only be seen by someone actually looking for them, it was all systems go. When she finally got them, she found out how much she had been missing. That first day, we went home and I put on Pink Floyd's *Dark Side of the Moon* for her. She said it was like hearing it properly for the first time and actually cried a little while listening to it.

Diane sometimes hated me for not having the kind of health problems she did. In fact, my teeth were in pretty bad shape but I was more afraid of dentists than she was. My stomach was never very good to me and my knees ached in wet weather and slowed me down. Now I too relied on a walking stick. But I never went through a fraction of what poor Diane did.

A couple of old wrecks

I know that Diane really missed our holidays in the warm sun. That Mediterranean sunshine was some of the best medicine she ever had. But one thing or another always seemed to keep us from a good old summer holiday. In addition to the better climate, those trips provided some of our very best times together and we would often reminisce about them, our memories aided by lots of photos and assorted little souvenirs scattered around the house. More than once, when we were in a place that we particularly loved, Diane would gaze at the beautiful scenery, let out a little sigh and quietly say: "You may bury me here." It became a standard joke – a slightly strange joke but one that reflected our feeling that we always left a little bit of ourselves behind when we reluctantly went home. I could not blame Diane for missing that feeling, one that I shared.

Well, we'll always have Paris, as Bogie said in *Casablanca* (I once tried saying "Here's looking at you, kid" to Diane but she just laughed). Thanks to the Eurostar, Paris became an easy yet desirable getaway and we tried to get there for a few days every year. We had been to Paris enough times to have been to the major tourist sights (we even spent a long weekend in Disneyland Paris which really brought out the child in us) so we could simply enjoy the romance of the city itself.

We stayed in apartments rather than hotels. These tended to be on the quirky side and located in residential rather than tourist areas so, for a few days, we felt like Parisians. One of the places we had always wanted to see was Pere Lachaise cemetery, the final resting place of so many famous people. It was vast and unlike any cemetery I had ever seen. The atmosphere was peaceful and oddly comforting. Diane even cried at the grave of Jim Morrison – not for Morrison himself, she said, but for the lost dreams of our youth he represented.

On our last trip to Paris we stayed in the hilly and evocative area of Montmartre. The highlight of our stay was an afternoon spent in Espace Dali, a compact museum devoted to the works of Salvador Dali but featuring mostly sculptures and ornaments rather than paintings. For Diane, this was a different kind of Disneyland and she took her time lingering over each piece and loving every minute of it. Her big brown eyes were as bright as I had ever seen them. I was reminded of a Dali quote: "I don't do drugs – I am drugs."

We were also becoming very familiar with Greenwich thanks to frequent trips to meet our friend Mary there, an event that Diane always looked forward to very much. In addition to long lunches in the Cutty Sark Café (we never went on the ship just to a small café a short distance away) we explored placed like the Painted Hall, the Maritime Museum and wandered all over Greenwich Park looking for a place to sit down. There were also little shops and a market in which the two women usually lost themselves. One time I went to a nautical shop on my own in search of yet another new hat and left Diane and Mary chatting happily on the steps by the great clipper ship. When I came back they were in friendly conversation with a tourist couple who turned out to be from Baltimore. They were not as interested in how I came to be living in England as they were by Mary's Irish accent.

Just because I have not mentioned hypos for a few pages does not mean they did not continue to happen. Because of them and the number of low blood tests in Diane's book (she did not always record the low ones), the local diabetic clinic and her GP both decided that a change in insulin might improve matters. There had been some changes in diabetic treatment over the years including insulin pumps and injection pens but Diane had always preferred to stick to the regimen she was familiar with and comfortable with. But these representatives of the NHS continued to pressure her into changing to something called analogue insulin.

This new and improved insulin was supposed to provide better control over sugar levels and required only a single injection every day, although this injection was more complicated. They painted such a rosy picture that Diane finally agreed to try it. We were both given a brief training in the injection method and given all the necessary supplies. I could tell that Diane had misgivings but she was told that if she continued to have hypos she would have no choice. So we took the stuff home and looked at it as though it was something that would turn Diane into Mr Hyde.

The doctor wanted Diane to start the new insulin on a Friday which was not very bright because if something went wrong over the weekend we would not be able to contact anyone. The practice nurse said she would ring us to check on the progress but she never did. Diane always injected at 7:30am and I told her to be sure to wake me so that I could help her or at least be there for moral support. The first injection seemed to be all right but it left Diane's sugar level higher than usual and never really came down. Saturday was even worse with Diane getting tests of almost 20 – when they should have been 6 to 8 – and not coming down. Diane always felt unwell when her sugar was high and now she was afraid to eat anything in case it went even higher. We had a very rough day and night.

On Sunday morning, Diane rashly decided to do the injection without waking me first. Not only did her sugar levels shoot up but she became dizzy and her heart was pounding. I found her in a terrible state and began to fear that I would have to ring for an ambulance. But the worst thing was that Diane was panicking and my first priority was to calm her down. This took a while but she eventually stabilised and the dizziness went away. Her sugar was still high and we wondered if the exercise of a long walk might help to bring it down even though she was still a bit shaky. The idea appealed to Diane ("Get me out of this f**king house!") and we set off slowly to Valentine Park.

The walk did her good. She continued to calm down and her sugar came down a little bit. Not surprisingly, she wanted a cigarette as we discussed what to do next. My feeling was that she should dump the analogue insulin and go back to the old stuff. Diane said that she wanted to talk to the doctor or the nurse first and would ring them first thing on Monday morning before doing an injection. In the event, neither doctor nor nurse had arrived when Diane called and she asked for one of them to ring her as soon as they came in. Diane waited as long as she could then injected with the old insulin. When the nurse finally rang, it was a case of informing her rather than asking permission. So much for that experiment.

After this episode, Diane promised that she would work harder and be more cooperative about keeping her sugar levels where they were supposed to be. And, for an unusually long time, she kept that promise. But I kept some of the analogue insulin to threaten Diane with should she ever falter.

But, sadly, worse was to come. Diane's mother, who was now well into her nineties, was becoming increasingly frail and her mental state was also worsening. Diane had given up trying to talk to her the phone because Annie would forget what she was doing and put the phone down in mid-sentence. Our visits to Glynn Court became less frequent because Diane found them too emotional and did not want to upset her mother unduly. Diane was also afraid that Annie would not realise who she was but on our last visit it was Diane who initially failed to recognise the frail woman in the common room.

The summer of 2019 had begun with the analogue insulin fiasco. As the summer was nearing its end, bad news started to come out of Fordingbridge. This news was sometimes confusing. First we heard that Annie had suffered a fall and been taken to hospital as a precaution. She was back at Glynn Court after a few days but then contracted a bug that was going around the care home. And, of course, her heart was always a concern. For some reason, communication with Lynne seemed difficult. Diane wanted to rush down there but we were unsure if Annie was at Glynn Court or in Salisbury Hospital. There was the additional problem of being unable to find a hotel room because it was the peak tourist season. I finally managed to book us into a new establishment and we prepared to go.

On the day we were scheduled to travel, we received an email from Lynne to say that Annie had passed away. Diane had missed her chance to say goodbye just as she had with her father. If anything, she was more devastated than before. We cancelled our reservation and decided not to go to Salisbury until it was time for the funeral which would not be for three weeks. In the meantime, I tried to my best to console Diane who was inconsolable.

Diane and her mother – the way she wanted to remember her

I had booked us a room above a recently renovated bistro a short walk from Salisbury Station. From there it was easy to get a taxi to take us to the crematorium. Lynne had arranged the entire ceremony. We sat quietly in the front row, Diane clutching my hand and trying to be brave. I cried a bit but not nearly as much as Diane. I could never underestimate the bond that existed between Diane and Annie – it was both spiritual and emotional. I had always been told that Annie and Ron were more like friends than parents but I was lucky enough to feel that they were both to me. I could only imagine what thoughts were running through Diane's mind. I do not think Diane ever loved anyone as completely and unreservedly as she did her mother – and that includes me.

Diane was never quite the same again. A bit of her sparkle seemed to be gone forever and she no longer laughed quite as easily – if she laughed at all. She almost seemed to have feelings of guilt although what she could possibly feel guilty about was unclear.

From Diane's notes dated Sunday 25 August 2019:

This is a week since Mummy died. It is surreal – nothing makes sense at the moment...I am not coping very well...My mind keeps skittering around. The child I was carrying at 17 would have been 52 this year. When Mummy found out I was nearly 5 months pregnant we had a "talk". Daddy seemed resigned? Mum was firstly a bit hysterical them calmed down enough to talk. She gave me a choice – to have an abortion or to have it. I knew she didn't want me to have a baby so I did the abortion. Not fun.

Mick didn't care and threw away 4 years of growing together. Our love did not survive. Such a long time ago.

Mummy I miss you so very much. I loved you so much while you were here. And I love you now. Mummy thank you for all the giggles and exciting things we have done. Thank you for your support when things went wrong. Thank you for bringing me up with ethics and thank you for being you. I promise to be a better person and try to look after David better...I love you Mum.

Getting back to something resembling normality was not going to be easy.

Diane had the usual round of appointments and decided to have a new set of dentures made – this time by a more qualified Italian dentist – to replace the ones that never seemed to fit properly. This was important because bad dentures restricted the kind of food she could handle and her meals did not always contain enough carbohydrates to keep her sugar up – and the last thing we needed at this point was hypos. Despite her efforts to find distractions, Diane remained depressed and was smoking a minimum of two packs of cigarettes a day. My efforts to help her had only limited results. Her GP suggested grief counselling but there was no appointment available for three months. So we basically coped on our own. It is hard in those circumstances to always find the right thing to say, even for someone who was allegedly good with words.

On our main calendar in the kitchen, Diane marked each Sunday with how many weeks it had been since Annie died. The changing season and shorter days did not help her mood. A trip to Greenwich was a rare bright spot but was soon followed by a hypo that required an ambulance. As Diane slowly regained consciousness she kept mumbling "Mum... Mummy..." I have seldom felt so helpless.

Winter was always the worst time of the year for Diane. She hated the short days and feeling cold. She still went for walks in the park in the morning, weather permitting – exercise with cigarettes. My attempts to lighten the mood were only occasionally successful. I regret that I left her on her own too much. Diane said I was anti-social but I simply did not know what else to do.

Gradually, things began to improve bit by tiny bit. We even talked about going to Paris in March for Diane's 70th birthday. Diane was slowly coming back. As we got into December, she began to talk about Christmas. We did not normally make a big fuss about the holiday but that year Diane wanted to. She asked for an advent calendar and I got her two – a pretty one and a funny one – as well as some silly Christmas crackers. Our old artificial tree had not been out of the loft for years so we decided to buy a little twelve inch live tree in a pot complete with tiny lights and gold stars. I was actually beginning to see a hint of joy in Diane's face.

We had long ago given up trying to buy each other presents – although we each occasionally cheated – and instead simply exchanged several cards. For Christmas dinner, we bought a turkey crown which Diane covered with bacon and cooked with roast potatoes. It lasted for three meals. On Christmas Day, we enjoyed our quiet dinner, pulled the entire box of crackers, and watched *National Lampoon's Christmas Vacation* – the only Christmas film Diane liked. No matter how many times she had seen it, she always giggled throughout. It was our best Christmas in years and the happiest Diane had been in months. I thanked the gods that I had got my darling wife back.

On New Year's, Diane gave me a card. The front of it had a typically New Age type painting of a pretty dancer in pink. On the inside, Diane wrote:

"My darling David –

I wish you happies, a lot of laughter and a whole lot of health for 2020.

Love is all around you,

From Diane xxxx"

Little did we know…

===

EIGHTEEN – GENTLY INTO THAT GOOD NIGHT

I wish I could conclude this story by saying that we lived happily ever after.

Diane passed away quietly in her sleep in the early hours of Monday 10 February 2020. It was completely unexpected. We had said goodnight as we always did around midnight on Sunday, a chilly day marked by gale force winds that had blown over the large honeysuckle bush in our garden. I remember that as I cuddled Diane for what was the last time she said softly: "That's nice." It is strange the things one remembers about such times.

I had been awakened by Diane's alarm clock at 7:30. This was not unusual as she frequently failed to hear it if she was sleeping on her good ear. I found her comfortably curled up in her favourite sleeping position. But when I tried to rouse her, I got no response. A quick look at her face told me something was wrong. I rang for an ambulance. The first thing the operators always asked was: "Is the patient breathing?" I could only reply: "I don't think so."

The operator told me to lay Diane on the floor on her back and to try to perform CPR on her by compressing her chest, I had seen this done in numerous films and television shows but it is not as easy as they make it look, especially when trying to do it to someone you love so much. The operator stayed on the phone until the ambulance arrived which was, thankfully, very quickly. Once the crew took over, I moved out of the way and into the den. At one point they asked me for a pillow and I gave them one off my bed but that was about all they said to me. For a long time, I just sat there and listened.

My initial thought was that this was some sort of really severe hypo but then I realised that Diane always cried out and thrashed about when having a hypo but she had looked quite cosy in her bed. As I listened to the attempts to revive her, it was obvious this was something more. Even so, I kept thinking that Diane would be revived and taken to hospital so I should start thinking about getting a few things together. But the crew kept repeating "no response" and I began to fear the worst. I don't know how long the ambulance crew worked on Diane but eventually one of them came into the den and said in a very professional voice: "Your wife is dead."

I have since come to believe that Diane was gone long before I found her and that nothing would have brought her back. The crew was obviously obligated to try but I think they knew it too.

Because it was an unexpected death at home, the police had to be called in to inspect the body, presumably for evidence of domestic violence or worse. While one officer carried out this mercifully brief investigation, a young female constable sat with me in the den and asked stupid questions. When they were finished, they said they would leave me alone with Diane to say goodbye.

Diane had been moved so that she partially lay on the landing with her legs over the doorway to the main bedroom. She was naked but had some sort of device in her mouth through which they had tried to insert a breathing tube. This made a final kiss impossible. There was some blood on the pillow and the carpet which was never explained. She looked very small and vulnerable but I kept thinking: this is not my Diane – my Diane is gone.

That night had been the first night of a full moon. Diane had always been superstitious about full moons and kept careful track of them. I never understood this but the belief seemed very real to her. Now I was starting to believe it myself.

A member of the crew came to tell me that an undertaker had been called and could I come downstairs to help them fill out the details for their report. As we were doing this, the postman peered through the door, obviously concerned about the emergency vehicles outside. I took the post from him and he said we could talk tomorrow. I went to the kitchen and helped with the obligatory paperwork. The next thing I knew, a pair of undertakers straight out of central casting arrived. I had no wish to see Diane being carried down the stairs in a body bag so I retreated to the garden for a few minutes. She was taken to the East Ham Mortuary where the coroner would conduct a post-mortem which is apparently a requirement in the case of a sudden and unexpected death.

This was the worst day of my life. While I can vividly recall much of it, the actual sequence of events and length of time are less certain. For some reason, I think it was all over by 9:30 and I was suddenly alone – very alone. After feeling numb for I do not know how long, I began to think that there were things I needed to do and people I should notify. Oddly enough, my first thought was to ring and cancel the flowers I had ordered for Diane for Valentine's Day. I was grateful they did not ask the reason. I then had to go through some of Diane's things to find a couple of phone numbers. In doing so, I opened the kitchen drawer that held most of her diabetic stuff. Well, sweetheart, I thought, you won't be needing that anymore.

I phoned our friend Mary who was quite shocked. Only a couple of days before she and Diane had exchanged emails about our next meeting. Then I rang Lynne, something I was almost afraid to do. We were not on best terms at that time and I expected a frosty reception. I think she asked if something was wrong with Diane and I blurted out "She's dead". From then on, any tension between us evaporated. I told both of them I would keep them informed of any developments as they occurred but this would be through emails as I was finding it difficult to keep my voice from breaking up.

The rest of the day is something of a blur. I know I cried a lot and carried around a small hand towel into which I frequently buried my face. If I ate anything, it was minimal. I actually made Diane's bed and put the nightdress she had originally been wearing under her pillows. The bed has remained like that ever since. I temporarily threw the bloodied pillow into a wardrobe to wash or dispose of later. There was a blood stain on the landing about four inches across. At first I could not bear to do anything about it and then it was too late. It became a constant reminder although, over the past year or so, it has nearly faded away. Everywhere I looked there were things belonging to Diane that I knew I would have to do something about – but not just yet. I was still trying to get my head around what had happened – a process that is still not complete. How or if I slept that night, I do not know.

Despite my own shock and emotional upset, I am eternally grateful that Diane passed away peacefully and apparently without pain in her own bed. We should all be that lucky. She looked so comfortable when I found her. I wonder if she knew what was happening or if she simply drifted off to sleep and never woke up. I only wish we had the chance to say goodbye instead of merely goodnight although I do not know if either of us could have really handled that.

I always used to think when someone died that they finally found out what happens afterwards – the great mystery. Lately I find myself wondering if anything happens at all. Just about everybody seems to hope, if not necessarily believe, that there is something. There is only one way of finding out. Woody Allen used to say: "I'm not afraid of death – I just don't want to be there when it happens." My own views about mortality seem to be evolving. If there was the tiniest chance of being with Diane again, I might forsake the habits of a lifetime and become an optimist. The worst thought is not thinking anymore.

I suddenly had lots to think about.

I could not make any definite arrangements until I heard from the coroner's office which I was told would be in two or three days. I hated to think of Diane being in that mortuary – she always hated being cold. I decided it was best to keep busy rather than think too much. The internet was seldom so useful. I found a site that offered a variety of remembrance and announcement cards and found a tasteful "In Loving Memory" card that I could mail to assorted friends to tell them what had happened. **Most responded with nice sympathy cards. I sent one of the cards to my brother Frank in Florida because he was the only member of my family that I had any sort of contact with. He rang me, we had a nice chat and he said that he would inform other members of the family. I was shocked when I later received a nice sympathy card and note from my sister Kathy. Brother Bob, of course, remained silent.**

Diane Kujawa
27 March 1950 - 10 February 2020

Diane passed away peacefully in her sleep
without warning under a full moon.
She is survived by David,
her husband of thirty-five years.

The service will be a private cremation

She left us too soon

My son Nick and I had not really communicated for some time but I sent him an email because I knew he had liked Diane. He was very saddened by the news – more so than I expected – and it led to a renewal of our email correspondence. I also had to cancel dentist and chiropodist appointments and explain why it would not be necessary to re-schedule but I decided that could wait until nearer the time.

Kenny the postman came back the next day and was really shocked by the news. He was an older guy that Diane had looked forward to seeing every morning. He called her "darling" and I jokingly referred to him as her boyfriend. Kenny said he would tell the other postmen on our route because all the ones who knew Diane liked her. That was the sort of effect she had on people.

Sorting out all of Diane's stuff was another matter and would take weeks if not months when I could bring myself to do it.

A couple of days later, I had a call from a nice lady at the coroner's office to tell me the gist of the post-mortem report. She read off some technical terms – which I would not remember until they appeared on the death certificate – and then tried to explain them. Diane's diabetes was only a secondary cause. The real culprits were *Ischaemic heart disease* and *Coronary artery atheroma.* In simple language, her arteries had become blocked which caused her heart to stop. This was the result of years of heavy smoking. Why it happened at that particular moment was unknown. As I tried to absorb this information, the nice lady told me the report would be forwarded to my local council with whom I would need to register Diane's passing and receive a death certificate. Not that it really mattered but I felt oddly relieved that the coroner had been female.

I would be lying if I did not feel a bit of anger at hearing this news. I was angry with Diane for having done this to herself, for resisting all advice and attempts to get her to do something about her smoking. And I was angry at myself for not trying harder. Anger is supposedly one of the stages of grief and fortunately mine passed very quickly. I loved Diane too much. But I regretted losing the extra years we might have had together.

Even before I had this report, I had begun to think about what would happen next. Nearly a year before, I had begun to quietly make arrangements for my own passing. This was prompted by several things: my not really wanting a funeral, my dislike of the British cemeteries I had seen, and being impressed by David Bowie's decision to have an efficient and unattended direct cremation. I felt if that was good enough for Bowie, it was good enough for me. The usual internet research brought me to a company called Pure Cremation who specialised in collecting the deceased, performing a dignified but unattended cremation, and either scattering the ashes in their garden of remembrance or returning them to whoever was specified. This all appealed to me especially since I thought, if I went first, my darling Diane would not be in any shape to deal with such things. So I signed up for it, paid for the service in full, and received, among other things, a card to carry with me containing all the necessary contact details for Pure Cremation in case I suddenly dropped dead.

It was a couple of months before I worked up the courage to tell Diane about this and, as expected, she was not pleased. I tried to explain my reasoning, but all she could say was: "So I won't be able to say goodbye to you." It was a valid point but who knew what the circumstance might be.

After a review of the services in and around Ilford, my thoughts kept returning to Pure Cremation. When I looked at their website again I found that they now offered the option of having a service in the smaller room of their new crematorium. For thirty minutes, up to twelve people could gather in the Oak Room to say goodbye. We could conduct any sort of service we wanted ourselves. Pure Cremation would provide a screen for a slide show of favourite photos and as well as playing two or three songs we selected. It sounded like the sort of ceremony Diane would have liked and there was the added advantage of this crematorium being located in Hampshire. I sort of consulted with Lynne but my mind was already made up.

I felt greatly relieved when Pure Cremation informed me that they had collected Diane from the mortuary and she was now "resting" at their facility in Hampshire. It would mostly be Diane's family attending the Saturday ceremony with our friend

Mary travelling with me by train from London. Diane used to joke about our possible funerals – "Who would come?" she would ask – now we knew. Both Lynne and I wrote eulogies while I emailed the photos for the slide show to Pure Cremation as well as my musical selections. It was very much a do-it-yourself ceremony but the sort of simple and low-key affair that I kept telling myself Diane would have approved of.

The Charlton Park crematorium, located in secluded grounds near Andover, was much nicer than the one in Salisbury and the compact Oak Room was a perfect setting. Diane's closed pine coffin rested at one end with several rows of seats facing it. There were some flowers and a few candles in front of windows that looked out onto the gardens. The screen was directly above the coffin and Hannah volunteered to work the remote for the music. I brought with me one of the little wooden cat-shaped tea light holders that Diane liked so much and placed it on the coffin with its black candle flickering.

Mary and I had taken a taxi from Andover station and were the first to arrive. We were greeted by a very kind and gently professional lady. Mary went to the ladies and as I stood there and looked around, it all suddenly hit me. I rushed into the gents and tried with only limited success to control myself. When I came out, the family had arrived. I had not seen them since Annie's funeral and it was not an easy reunion. The lady then directed us to the Oak Room.

We began by listening to Joni Mitchell's *Songs to Aging Children Come* which Diane liked a lot and seemed somehow appropriate. The other song was perhaps not the best – The Rolling Stones' *You Can't Always Get What You Want.* We had once seen that played at a funeral in a film called *The Big Chill* and Diane had remarked she wanted it for her funeral. But I later realised that a much better choice would have been Bob Dylan's *Forever Young* which Diane loved and would probably have been more suitable to the occasion. In my defence, I can only say that my thoughts were not always clear at that time.

I had written what I felt was a lovely eulogy for Diane but I knew that, in my present state, I would be unable to read it aloud no matter how much I wanted to. So Charlotte and Hannah read it for me, each taking a page, while I could only listen. Lynne's eulogy was more controlled but also very warm, especially her memories of her and Diane's childhood years. There was an amazing amount of love in that room. After everyone had said goodbye to Diane they left me alone with her for a few minutes. I still cannot remember those moments without emotion.

Afterwards, Lynne and Brian took Mary and me to the station. Very little was said on the train but a lot of thinking was going on. I said goodbye to Mary at Waterloo Station and made my way home. It was dark when I got there. I had hardly eaten all day but could not face cooking anything. Instead I ordered a bunch of chicken nuggets and fries from Burger King. It was not an easy night to get through.

The nice lady from Pure Cremation had told me the actual cremation would take place on Monday morning. About ten days later, her ashes were delivered – Diane, in a sense, had come home. In just a couple of weeks it would have been Diane's 70th birthday. I had ordered what I considered to be a simple yet stylish metal urn (bought online, of course). What a weird experience it was to transfer the ashes from their very functional carrier to their final resting place. I put the urn on the top shelf of a bookcase in Diane's bedroom. I gradually added some candles, a picture and artificial flowers that began to look like a little shrine. But it was a better focal point than a tombstone in a crowded cemetery and I soon found myself saying "good morning" and "goodnight" to Diane every day and occasionally talking to her.

I also have a small heart-shaped container which holds a few of Diane's ashes and which I keep on my desk. I often pick it up and just hold it for a minute or two which I find comforting. One of these days I would like to discreetly scatter just a small handful of Diane's ashes in Pere Lachaise in Paris. I think she would really like that.

I was still kept busy sorting out things like pensions, bank accounts and fulfilling Diane's wishes from her will. Some of this was easier than expected. When I had registered her passing at the town hall, I was able to sign up for the "Tell Me Once" plan which notified authorities such as the passport office, the election commission, even the bus pass people for me. I also started to think that I needed a new will since I had more or less intended to leave everything to Diane.

No sooner were the legalities and paperwork sorted out than a little thing called Covid-19 reared its ugly head. Soon there were lockdowns and grocery shortages and all kinds of stuff to make any possible return to a sort of normal life impossible. I found myself feeling almost grateful that Diane had missed all of it because she would have felt especially vulnerable and tense. It meant that 2020 was going to be a terrible year in more ways than one – and that one was bad enough.

I suppose what I am living now could be called my leftover life. Self-isolation was not a problem for me, even though I never had any symptoms, because I was living alone anyway with just a stupid cat that was no company or comfort whatsoever. A kind of routine gradually took over. I tried to be a good boy and do things that Diane would have wanted me to do like washing up after every meal, making my bed, doing laundry on a fairly regular basis and even getting the hoover out from time to time. When summer came, I tried to keep Diane's beloved garden as tidy as possible. I also started to collect little remembrance items – as if I could ever forget Diane – and lit a candle for her in the kitchen every evening as I prepared my dinner.

In early January, Diane had arranged to have a memorial tree planted in Valentine Park for her parents. It was something she was very anxious to do but, sadly, she did not live long enough to see it. But it made me decide to have a tree planted for her. Unfortunately, the tree planting season in the park was at the end of the year so I would have to wait to arrange it. But by December the tree and plaque were in place in a spot that faced the boating lake near where we first entered the park together.

I wish that Diane had written a book that told our story from her point of view. I know from her letters that she had a flair for expressing herself. But whenever I suggested that she write down some of her memories or impressions, she always seemed reluctant, usually making a joke about her faulty or incomplete memory. I think that, unlike me, Diane did not like to reflect on the past too much apart from some cherished memories. She was also somewhat ambivalent about the future. For Diane, it was always the present that mattered and she wanted to make the most of it. I sometimes wonder if I occasionally helped or hindered that ambition.

In those far-off days when Diane and I were just pen friends, we used to make cassette tapes to send to one another. These contained some of our favourite music interspersed with us talking. Some of it was similar to our letters but we also shared memories, explained the habits of our respective countries, told jokes, even recited the odd bit of poetry.

One highlight was Diane's attempt to tell a slightly naughty joke. It was just after she had moved into her flat and her mother was with her – both obviously a bit tipsy. Diane struggled with the joke, with audible prompting from Mummy, in between collapsing in giggles. It was a terrible joke but an utterly delightful performance.

At some point, I re-recorded Diane's tapes onto another cassette, this time transferring just the bits of Diane talking. The ninety minute tape was in chronological order and reflected our growing relationship. Diane gradually became less nervous and more natural (she hated using a microphone). The later tapes became more personal in anticipation of my first visit.

I have managed, after much searching, to finally locate this tape. So for the first time in nearly eighteen months, I was able to hear Diane talking to me again. It was wonderful to listen to her familiar laughter and extremely emotional to hear her saying that she loved me.

About a year after we were married the BBC broadcast a six part drama serial called *Edge of Darkness* that Diane became inexplicably obsessed with. It had a typical BBC storyline in which the government and big business were the enemies of the people whose plans could only be thwarted by a couple of mavericks. It was saved by good dialogue and good acting. Diane watched it numerous times on video and DVD until she practically knew the thing by heart. One aspect of the story was the murder of the main character's daughter early in the first episode. But as the series progressed, she kept making her presence felt, first by voice and then seemingly in person. I think it was this idea of a loving haunting that fascinated Diane and she sometimes used to joke that she would haunt me one day. I only wish that were true. If I cannot be with Diane, I would love to be haunted by her.

NINETEEN – BITS AND PIECES

Additional thoughts and memories:

Diane was fond of quoting Eliza from *My Fair Lady* in her best Cockney accent: "I'm a good girl, I am."

==========

Lynne wrote this to me in an email on Diane's birthday 2021: "I don't know if I ever told you but my earliest memory at the age of only two and a half was my Mum coming home with baby Diane. It was a sunny day and a few of the family came to see her. Mum bought me a toy broom and I went out in the garden to sweep the terrace. I was a bit disappointed cause everyone had told me how exciting it would be when they came home but all I saw was a little bundle fast asleep and I wasn't allowed to touch her. However, it pleases me to think that her arrival is my earliest memory and it must therefore have been a very important event."

==========

Diane's family had a charming custom when taking pictures of each other. Instead of telling the person or persons being photographed to say "cheese", they were told to say "sex". This not only produced big smiles but also an occasional giggle. It explains why they all look so happy in their photos.

==========

One day, Diane and another girl decided to play hooky from school. Of course, they were found out. When questioned, instead of inventing some typically ridiculous schoolgirl excuse, Diane simply shrugged and said: "We wanted to see the tennis." Apparently, this unexpected bit of honesty caused everyone to laugh.

==========

Diane and I loved to share the experiences of our wildly different childhoods. One story she told me was when her mother was working as a seamstress in the East End garment district. One day, or possibly more than one day, she took Diane to work with her, presumably because there was no one to look after her. Even then, Diane was ever willing to help anyone who needed it. She endeared herself to some of the other women who were earthy Cockney types. They thought it was highly amusing to get Diane to say words like "fuck" in her cute little voice. Diane thought it was funny – needless to say: Mummy was not amused.

==========

The biggest mistake of my life was marrying Jackie. The best thing I ever did was to marry Diane.

==========

I vividly recall the moment I first realised how addicted to cigarettes Diane was. In August 1983 we had gone to the Barbican to see the RSC production of *Cyrano de Bergerac* with Derek Jacobi. That had always been one of my favourite plays and since we had earlier seen and enjoyed Jacobi in *Much Ado About Nothing,* it was an evening to look forward to. As usual, we got to the theatre just in time. As the first act progressed, I was aware of Diane becoming increasingly restless. At first I thought her sugar might be low but when I asked if she was all right, she snapped at me – possibly for the first time in our relationship. The fidgeting and sighing continued until the intermission. Even before the lights had come up, Diane was up and heading for the lobby. Once there, she lit a cigarette which she inhaled with deep satisfaction. She had two or three cigarettes in quick succession – as many as the intermission would allow – and was suddenly her usual happy self again. She greatly enjoyed the second act and even cried at the end. And I got a little apology. I learned a valuable lesson: If we were going somewhere in which smoking was not permitted, always allow time for a couple of cigarettes before entering. Needless to say, as time went on and smoking was increasingly banned, this was not always easy to achieve. But I learned to recognise the "I need a fag" look and, to my eternal shame and regret, I did what I could to make it possible.

==========

Diane's time with Gerry certainly left a few psychological scars but she also retained a kind of affection either for Gerry himself or that period in her life which she often talked about or, more likely, a combination of both. Diane regarded being married to me as something safe but I think there were occasions when she found being safe a tad boring. Diane's emotions were nothing if not complicated and I am convinced she had thoughts that she chose not to share with anyone, including me. Some of these thoughts she scribbled into small notebooks that I only discovered after her death. I am sure she never meant anyone to read them. But as surprising as some of these reflections were – surprising but not really shocking – it is safe to assume that they only hinted at some of the contemplations that were hidden in a secret corner of her mind.

==========

Diane's ex-husband Gerry featured in a news item in 2013. He had been living on a 24ft boat on the Essex coast. At age 65, he decided to sail this boat by himself across the Atlantic to South America where he heard there was a sunken Nazi U-boat filled with gold. However, he set off in bad weather and was blown into Eastbourne harbour by strong winds where he ran aground. He refused all help and even threatened the Coast Guard with a flare gun. The police were called who subdued him and took him to a hospital for mental health checks. He was released after a few days, did not return to his boat, and promptly disappeared. I only found this story on the internet after Diane had passed away. She would no doubt have smiled wryly and said something like: "Oh, yes, that's Gerry all right."

==========

We used to celebrate – or, at least, to mark – October 26th as Diane's Second Birthday. Now that I think about it, it would probably have been more accurate to call it her Re-Birth Day because her life – and Diane herself – was never the same after that day. I only wish she could have had a third birthday. For a long time while the ambulance crew worked to revive her, I honestly thought they would succeed and we would be going to the hospital. I suppose you have to be optimistic in those circumstances although deep down inside I must have known that Diane's life – and, in a way, my life – was over. When reality became apparent, I felt an internal numbness that has never totally gone away to this day.

==========

There is a line when King Lear is mourning Cordelia and he says: "She is gone forever." That line really hit me with its finality. I heard it unexpectedly in the Vincent Price film *Theatre of Blood* and it suddenly affected me very much. Forever had never seemed like such a long time before. I suppose sooner or later I will also be gone forever. Did it really matter that we were here?

==========

I never knew I had so many tears.

==========

Sunday 20 March 2022

Today is the spring equinox – the first day of spring and, as luck would have it, it is a bright sunny day although with a slight nip in the air. When I went into the kitchen to put some lunch together, I looked out the window and the wildly overgrown garden. The mild winter and too much rain had made everything grow into a sort of jungle. Out in the garden was Diane's bench where she loved to sit and read and soak up the warm sun – it was her favorite spot. All the rain had left a puddle on the seat of the bench. I noticed something moving there. It was a small robin having a bath in the puddle. He was having a wonderful time. I do not think I have seen a robin in nearly two years. I remembered the superstition about robins being spiritual messengers. So there was this robin enjoying itself on Diane's bench in Diane's garden on a sunny day. I felt quite touched by the symbolism. It would be nice to think that there was some truth to the superstition.

Update 5 July – I have seen a robin in the garden several times, often just after I have cut the grass and it comes down to forage. Today was slightly different. Once again, I was looking out the kitchen window. There is a garden chair right in front of the window. As I stood there, a robin flew down the garden and landed on the back of the chair. It looked straight at me through the window – we could not have been more than twenty-four inches apart. We looked at one another for about half a minute. Then, just as suddenly, the robin took off – the proverbial flying visit. I was very glad to see the robin. I had been in a strange mood after having a couple of very strange and unsettling dreams. Somehow, the robin seemed reassuring.

===

TWENTY – DIANE'S STORIES

Diane occasionally took a stab at writing little stories in her own wonderful style. Here are three of them, two of which I never saw until after she was gone.

A story:

She lay on her side with one arm and one leg twisted sinuously about the pillow which she had, unconsciously during the night, slid down from the top of the bed to beneath the quilt. "Oh, well," she sighed to herself upon hearing the first wails of music from the radio-alarm, "it was better than nothing" although she really secretly despised herself for her weakness in that the inability to sleep unless she had something cuddled in her arms had made her turn to a feather pillow. She turned on her back and stretched every inch in a long muscle cracking movement then say up and opened her eyes to the misty steams of light trying to struggle through the curtains hung against the windows. She blinked, a long pause and then blinked again as if to ensure that she really was awake. After ascertaining it to be fact rather than fiction she reached out for the inevitable cigarette which always lay in wait next to the huge box of matches and ashtray on the side of the bed. Having lit a cigarette – and fumbled on her glasses – she thought about the day. Whatever would happen today – not a lot more than happened any other day she supposed – the office would still be there, the same people as every other day would still be there – but what really was the point of it all.

Suddenly, a small flash of pain impinged itself upon her consciousness – the cigarette had burned down right to the end and had just begun to burn her fingers. With a muffled oath she threw it into the ashtray with an angry movement. "Serves her right," she thought, "should be sitting daydreaming." With an impatient shrug at herself she threw on an old faded blue wrap and headed for the bathroom in anticipation of a long hot shower to take the night away from mind and body.

She heard the harsh strident tone of the telephone and, grabbing a bath sheet which seemed to wrap itself around her legs in a wicked way designed to trip her up, she flew into the sitting room to pick up the receiver only to hear the steady brrrr as someone put the phone down the other end. She waited and sure enough it rang again within the minute. She picked it up and waited, not saying anything. Not because she did not want to say anything but because she knew who it would be and wanted to hear his light American voice before she said anything. "Hello, my love – it's David." "Hello," she said, trying to keep the quiver out of her voice, "how are you?"

It was a bit of a rhetorical question – as it always was.

~~~~~~~~~~~~~~~~~~~~

Another story:

The usual dim lights used to obscure the general tattiness of the décor which resembles mock Greek peasantry. The odour of cheap food dressed to appease the eye but not the appetite wafting across the pocket-sized dance floor. The hour is yet too early for many people to have decided they will not score at the wine bars or pubs to have almost desperately made their way into the cellar. A few middle-aged, slightly seedy looking men stand at the bar with half-pints in hand waiting for their prey to make an appearance. Three women a little past their prime make their coy way to the ladies toilets to primp in readiness for any action which may await them.

The band which never quite made it (after having done the pub circuit back in their more reckless youthful days) strikes up the first of their middle of the road pop songs. There is none of the brashness or naïve banter that they used to do; this is the maturity that has bred a respectability of everything they perform now.

The two girls who always sit at the front of the dance floor now stand and begin their gyrations more or less in time with the music purely for the benefit of the band whose indifference never wavers. The girls know they stand no chance but it has become part of the ritual of their lives that still they endeavour to catch the eye of the man of their dreams who plays just for them each Saturday night. Perhaps tonight will be the night.

The man sat in a corner nursing his drink has seen it all before and looks on with an amused cynical eye – his thoughts wandering between the thought that he really should be working and concentrating on the quite attractive girl(?) woman(?) sat at an angle from him in the next booth. She looked quite and sat staring into middle-distance with a slightly dreamy expression. She certainly was not pretty he decided but had about her a certain aura that gave him the feeling that she did not belong in the place. Having made up his mind to take a chance he approached her table to stand diffidently before her. She looked up at him with a faint smile. Without speaking he held out his hand to her and she took it with a clumsiness that he found quite endearing. They collected coats and walked through the mass of people who had accumulated around the door. Once out in the crisp night air they walked slowly along Oxford Street, the bright lights on the trees and in shop windows giving the appearance almost of fairy land. The conversation between them flowed easily, the silences comforting, the occasional banter light and happy. The station was fairly empty and they smiled at each other conspiratively as they passed the young busker with his guitar who sang his favourite Eagles song in the subway. The strains of the song followed them down to the platform and they began to run to the train waiting there. Holding hands and laughing breathlessly they just jumped onto the train as the doors were about to close.

They sat on the train until it had gone round the Circle Line three times before they agreed it was time they actually went somewhere, like home for instance. She asked that he go with her to her home and he readily accepted. Anything was better than his own apartment.

Her place was something of an enigma to him as indeed she was. Without speaking, once they were inside, she went to the bedroom and he followed her. They stood looking at each other, their thoughts their own until the anticipation and excitement between them had built into an almost tangible reality. And so it began. Very gently he reached out and touched her hair, her face, and let his hand slip down the length of her body. With a sinuous movement the dress she wore was discarded. She wore nothing beneath it – but before her could fully appreciate the delicacy of her slender figure she turned and slid beneath the covers of the bed. He laughed while struggling out of his clothes and the sight of his antics brought soft giggles from her as she hid her face in the pillows. The glow of the lamp was enough for him to see that she enjoyed the sun judging from paleness of her skin around her hips as he pulled the covers from beneath her chin. Pictures began to form in her mind as they moved together. The movements being rather more natural than practised, each knowing and understanding the needs of the other. Their climax, when it came, was simultaneous. For long moments afterwards they stayed in the same position looking deeply into each other's eyes searchingly with childlike wonder. He was amazed when he saw tears forming in her eyes and held her close until the mood passed. When it had, they slept still with arms wrapped around each other.

The morning was heralded with the sound of bottles being rattled by the milk float in the street below but the couple wrapped in their dreams and warmth did not stir to the interruption of the quiet Sunday. When they did awake it was well into the day and the lady, after having made the usual pot of coffee, warmed the croissants in the oven and carrying the tray into the bedroom felt the same happiness that swept through her whenever she looked at her husband.....

~~~~~~~~~~~~~~~~~~~

Another story:

(This one, I assume, was a recollection of how Diane first met her supposed soulmate Gerry.)

There was a lady and let's call her, for the sake of this narrative, Janie. She was quite young – young in body years, about 28, old within her own mind. Married and lonely, the loneliness of insecurity was what troubled her at times especially when she was at home waiting, always waiting, for the time for her life to be fulfilled. This particular night was no worse and no better than any other to date. In fact, she thought, it was a bit better tonight. At least the radio was offering something in the way of light entertainment instead of the usual mind-screwing banalities. Some sound other than the music filtered through which she recognised as the front door being violently assaulted. Cursing under her breath, she walked out of the sitting room and down the hallway to open it. The fellow standing outside was only remarkable insofar as he looked like a refugee. Small, thin and with a bedraggled air about him as he peered myopically through thick-lensed glasses. He rather desperately clutched a handful of tickets in his right hand whilst his left nervously scratched his sparse beard.

"Yes?" she enquired a bit sharply.

"Er, do you want some tickets for the Youth Club raffle – only 50p each?" he stammered.

"Oh, ok. You'd better come in while I find my purse. If I leave the door it shuts because of the spring at the top and I don't like leaving people standing on the doorstep," she explained.

He followed her into the sitting room and looked around as she shook coins out of her purse onto the ironing board where she had been working at the clothes which were piled in a tidy heap on the table.

"Yours is the first place I've gone to tonight where the TV hasn't been blaring out a dumb soap opera," he remarked.

"I like music, especially rock. And when I'm doing mundane jobs it helps not to think too much. Hawkwind, Pink Floyd, Roxy, Led Zeppelin. Who do you like?" She looked at him quizzically, uncertain as to whether she liked him or not but glad of the diversion his appearance had created.

"I've got some good Hawkwind albums if you would like to come over some evening. We can have a chat and listen to some music."

She nodded at this invitation but proffered no verbal reply. After paying him for five tickets she went with him to the door and without a word of goodbye opened it to let him go on his way. As he walked along the hallway between the flats he heard her door slam shut with finality.

Janie sighed as she lit another cigarette and, cursing under her breath, she poured another scotch from the half-empty bottle which she always kept stashed in her kitchen cupboard. She drank and then jumped involuntarily at another unexpected rap on the front door. Nerves still jingling, she nearly ran to open the door again. There he was – looking even more decrepit than the first time. With a doleful expression he was raking through his pockets searching for only he knew what.

"Did I leave my tickets on your table?" was his anxious enquiry.

Laughing because he looked a little like a demented clown, she told him that she thought he was crazy and, no, there were no tickets other than those she had bought on her table.

"It's ok – I've found them!" he exclaimed and turned to go.

As he turned, she found herself saying: "If the offer of coffee and music was serious, I may well take you up on it one evening. Also, if the Youth Club needs any help, I'll be glad to offer my services."

He looked surprised but not unpleased. "Come over to the clubhouse any Tuesday or Thursday night. We could do with someone to help out."

So that was, in some measure, a beginning. It was also an ending. A beginning in the sense of a kind of freedom. An ending, as it were, of an era.

GALLERY

Pencil drawing by Diane

===

==

==

==

==

===

===

===

===

====================================

====================================

==

==

==

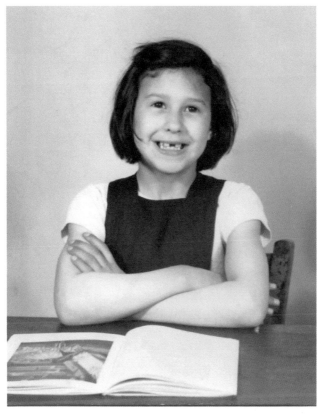

==

==

==

==

==

==

==

==

==

==

==

==

==

==

==

=======================================

=======================================

==

==

==

==

Printed in Great Britain
by Amazon